Grand Tour

Seeing the World

Anthony Sellick　James Bury　Kaori Horiuchi

新たな時代への扉

JN062936

SEIBIDO

photographs by
iStockphoto
Open Bionics
読売新聞社

音声ファイルのダウンロード／ストリーミング

CD マーク表示がある箇所は、音声を弊社 HP より無料でダウンロード／ストリーミングすることができます。下記 URL の書籍詳細ページに音声ダウンロードアイコンがございますのでそちらから自習用音声としてご活用ください。

http://seibido.co.jp/ad607

Grand Tour – Seeing the World

PREFACE

During the 17th and 18th centuries, wealthy young people took a trip around Europe in order to complete their education. This was called the Grand Tour. They visited famous historical sites, learned languages, and made friends with people in various countries. The Grand Tour helped prepare them for life as international citizens.

The Grand Tour series of books looks at a variety of important trends that are shaping the modern world. Each book examines issues that affect our lives, which will change our lives in the future, and which you will influence in the future.

The topics covered in the essays range widely and are grouped into four sections: the worlds of culture and society, science and technology, business and economics, and politics and international relations. Included are topics that encourage you to look at an everyday thing from a new perspective, topics that showcase the amazing progress and discoveries that are being made, and topics which focus on aspects of the world that need to be changed or which are changing too slowly.

We hope that you will find these topics interesting and thought-provoking, and that they encourage you to learn more about them. We sincerely hope you enjoy your Grand Tour.

Anthony Sellick, James Bury, and Kaori Horiuchi

CONTENTS

Business and Economics

Politics and International Relations

Chapter 1

I Don't Know What to Believe

Finding Truth Among Online Lies

▶ Useful Words

Choose a word from the list below to complete each sentence.

1. The typhoon was _____. Every building in town was damaged or destroyed.

2. A(n) _____ claimed he saw a ghost at our school. We were shocked when we saw the story reported on the television news.

3. You must go to the new ramen restaurant. Its Super Spicy Ramen is _____!

4. I left my phone on the train. Luckily, a(n) _____ person handed it in at the station.

5. My friend Shahida is a Muslim, but I'm not _____ at all.

> religious   trustworthy   devastating   hoaxer   extraordinary

▶ Reading

① 02~08

02 CD

1 The internet allows us to access more accurate information than at any other time in history. It also exposes us to more misinformation than at any other time in history. As well as the journalists who want to inform us and the educators who want to teach us, there are the politicians who want your vote, the
5 foreign governments who want to control your vote, the religious who want you to believe as they do, the bigots who want you to hate as they do, the companies who want your data and your money, the criminals and scammers who want your data and your money, the satirists who want to make you laugh, the hoaxers

who want to trick you, the confused, and the mentally ill. How can we tell if
10 something is a true story, propaganda, an advertisement, a con, a hoax, a joke, or
the delusions of someone who is mentally ill? Fortunately, the philosophical
tools of critical thinking, the methods of science, and the investigative tools of
journalism can help us to find the truth in a post-truth world.

03 CD

2 Philosophy provides us with the laws of
15 logic that allow us to analyze and appraise ideas.
However, just because an idea is logical does not
mean it is true. Fortunately, philosophy also gives
us a useful definition of truth: the truth of a
statement or an idea depends on how well it fits
20 with reality. Science focuses on the study of
reality and teaches us that we should disbelieve
an idea until we have evidence that supports it.
Furthermore, the amount of evidence we need to
believe an idea depends on the claim that is
25 being made. The cosmologist Carl Sagan
summarized this very well when he said that
"extraordinary claims require extraordinary
evidence." Like philosophy and science,
journalism also teaches us that any idea or claim
30 should be questioned, and that the sources of
any claim or idea must also be examined.

Fake news can be dangerous.

04 CD

3 For example, if your friend tells you that they have a pet dog, should you
believe them? Owning a pet dog is not uncommon, and if your friend is usually
reliable or trustworthy, you probably do not need any more evidence than their
35 word. Furthermore, you can ask your friend (and other friends) for details about
the dog, and you can easily visit your friend to see the dog for yourself. As a
result, you should probably believe your friend. However, if a stranger tells you
that they also have a pet dog, and that their dog is invisible, can fly, and enjoys
watching kabuki plays, you should demand a huge amount of evidence before
40 you believe that they have such an amazing, world-changing dog. Let's consider
some real-world examples.

05 CD

4 Many people use social media to communicate with their friends. However, many people also form friendships that are wholly online. This can be very dangerous because fake social media profiles are very common. Between 45 September 2018 and March 2019, Facebook alone deleted more than 3 billion fake profiles. Many criminals use fake social media profiles to contact people, which is known as catfishing. Financial criminals often use online dating profiles to begin a romance and then trick their victims into giving them money. In 2018, more than 20,000 people lost more than $140 million in just the US. More 50 disturbingly, sex criminals often target children and teenagers in order to obtain private pictures and videos which they then sell online. The emotional and psychological impact of being the victim of such crimes can be absolutely devastating. How much should we trust an online friend? Not much, because if you have not met a person in real life, then you have no idea who that person 55 really is.

06 CD

5 Millions of people around the world have watched videos online explaining that the world is not round but flat. What would it mean if it were true? First, it would mean that many of 60 our ideas about history, geography, and science are wrong. Secondly, it would mean that hundreds of thousands of people, including pilots, sailors, politicians, military leaders, and scientists, are all lying to us. As a result, we 65 should expect an enormous amount of high-quality evidence, and not just some YouTube videos and websites.

Some people think the world is flat. Could they be right?

07 CD

6 Believing incorrect ideas can have serious consequences. In Japan in 2013, nearly 70 70 percent of girls received the HPV vaccine, which can prevent a form of cancer that kills nearly 3,000 Japanese women every year. However, the proportion of girls getting the vaccine dropped to below 1 percent by 2015 because people opposed to vaccines spread false information about the safety of the HPV vaccine.

7 The examples above show us the dangers of being wrong. As a result, we
75 should use the tools that philosophy, science, and journalism give us to
investigate the claims and ideas we are exposed to every day. A good rule to
follow is this: the more it will cost you to be wrong, the more you should do to
ensure that you are right.

Notes

scammer「詐欺師」**con**「ペテン、嘘」**a post-truth world**「ポスト真実の世界」ポスト真実とは、客観的な真実よりも感情的な訴えや個人的信条が世論や政治に影響を及ぼす状況を意味する。そのような風潮がみられる世界のこと。アメリカのトランプ政権発足やイギリスの EU 離脱をめぐる論争を反映した用語。**cosmologist**「宇宙科学者」**Carl Sagan**「カール・セーガン（1934-1996）」アメリカの天文学者、作家。宇宙に関するドキュメンタリー番組を制作し、司会も務めた。**world-changing**「世界を変えるような」**catfishing**「キャットフィッシング、なりすまし」catfish は元々「ナマズ」を意味する。インターネット上で個人情報を偽り、相手を騙す行為。**dating profiles**「出会い系プロフィール」デートを目的として作られた人物紹介。**the HPV vaccine**「子宮頸がん予防ワクチン」HPV（**= human papillomavirus**）は子宮頸がんの原因とされるヒトパピローマウイルスの略語。

❯ Questions for Understanding

Part 1 *Look at the following statements about the passage. Write T if the statement is True, and F if it is False. Write the number of the paragraph where you find the answer in the parenthesis.*

1) ____ According to the passage, it is not always easy to identify whether online information is true or false. ( )

2) ____ The passage informs us that we should assume that an idea is true if it is logical. ( )

3) ____ We should think carefully before forming a friendship on social media. ( )

4) ____ Thinking about what the world would be like if an idea was true can be a helpful way to uncover the truth. ( )

Part 2 *Look at the following questions about the passage. Check the best answer for each.*

1) Which word has the closest meaning to the word "appraise" in Paragraph 2 (line 15)?
a. ☐ estimate   b. ☐ evaluate   c. ☐ rate   d. ☐ approve

2) According to the passage, what is "catfishing"?
- a. ☐ Deleting somebody's social media profile in order to bully them
- b. ☐ Creating a fake social media profile as a joke
- c. ☐ Using a fake social media profile for illegal activities
- d. ☐ Posting fake information on your social media profile

3) What does the passage imply regarding the spread of misinformation about the HPV vaccination?
- a. ☐ The HPV vaccine will gradually become more popular.
- b. ☐ Some Japanese women will die unnecessarily.
- c. ☐ Boys will start to receive the HPV vaccine in Japan.
- d. ☐ The HPV vaccine will become more expensive.

4) Which of the following is the key theme of the passage?
- a. ☐ It is easy to find useful and accurate information on the internet.
- b. ☐ It is easy to study science, philosophy, and journalism online.
- c. ☐ We should never trust the internet because people spread misinformation.
- d. ☐ Checking whether information is correct is everybody's responsibility.

❯ Summary

① 09 CD

Fill each space with the best word from the list below.

consequences	misinformation	investigative
accurate	exposed	bigots

For many of us today the internet is our primary source of information. Using it, we can rapidly find 1) _____ information about nearly any subject. However, there is also a huge amount of 2) _____ from satirists, criminals, and 3) _____ . The 4) _____ of being fooled and accepting untrue information as true can be very serious, and potentially deadly. How can we make sure that the information we are 5) _____ to is correct? Fortunately, the traditional 6) _____ techniques developed by philosophers, scientists, and journalists can still help us find the truth among a sea of lies.

▶ Over to You

Choose ONE of the statements below. Prepare a short response giving your opinion.

- **Social media companies should check whether information is true or not.**
- **Newspapers and magazines are more reliable than the internet.**

....

....

....

....

It's a Hikikomori World

Why Do Some People Withdraw from Society?

❯ Useful Words

Choose a word from the list below to complete each sentence.

1. The money he had was not _____ even though he had saved for a year.

2. I have two _____, a brother and a sister.

3. The doctor _____ her with influenza and told her to stay in bed for a few days.

4. I'm going to go shopping in Shibuya. Would you like to _____ me?

5. We should not be surprised that many librarians have _____ personalities.

| siblings | accompany | introverted | sufficient | diagnosed |

❯ Reading

① 10~16 CD

10 CD

1 Sometimes we just need to get away from it all. We need some time alone, a time when we can ignore our phones, email, and messages, and
5 escape from all the stresses and strains of life and other people. For most of us a long hike in the mountains, a relaxing soak in a hot spa, or a couple of days spent watching movies,

What can you do if society is too much?

¹⁰ television, or playing computer games is sufficient to leave us feeling refreshed and ready to re-engage with the world. However, for some people this is not enough, and they can find themselves seeking ever greater solitude until they are almost completely alone. These are the hikikomori.

2 While people suffering from acute social withdrawal were first described ¹⁵ in 1978 by Japanese researcher Kasahara Yoshimi, the word "hikikomori" was coined by Japanese psychiatrist Saito Tamaki in 1998. Generally, someone is considered to be a hikikomori if they have withdrawn into their home for more than six months and do not participate in society, for example by attending school or working. In this way, hikikomori are regarded as different to people ²⁰ who are shy, introverted, or who are suffering from social anxiety.

3 Hikikomori tend to be male (about one third of hikikomori are female), often have no siblings, commonly have a difficult relationship with one or both of their parents, and generally begin their withdrawal from society when they are teenagers. Many have experienced bullying or had problems forming friendships ²⁵ during their school years. After school, problems entering work are often reported by hikikomori. In addition, since hikikomori must depend on others – usually their parents – to finance their lifestyle, they tend to be from middle-class families. Furthermore, about half of hikikomori also have experience of mental illness other than social withdrawal. Surveys by the Japanese Cabinet ³⁰ Office in 2015 and 2018 found that there are about 541,000 hikikomori between the ages of 15 to 39, and 613,000 between the ages of 40 and 64. This means that about 1.2 percent of Japanese people are hikikomori.

4 While there are many positive aspects to our modern lives, we often find ourselves under a lot of competing pressures. For example, we are expected to ³⁵ perform well at school so that we can enter a good university, and we are expected to enter a good university so that we can get a good job. Advertising and social media constantly tell us that we should have perfect looks, own the latest goods, and be living perfect Instagrammable lives. However, not everybody can enter a first-rate school, university, or job, especially during economic ⁴⁰ downturns. Nor can everybody look like a model or live the life of a celebrity. In fact, the images of models that we see are often very different from how those models look in reality, and many celebrities are not rich. In other words, it is

impossible to meet all of these expectations. Trying, and failing, to achieve these impossible ideals is the root cause of mental illness in many people, including
45 depression, social anxiety, school withdrawal, and anorexia. Some people simply give up trying to meet the expectations of society and completely withdraw from it instead. These are the people with hikikomori syndrome.

14 **CD**

5 Because hikikomori syndrome was first described in Japan, it was
50 initially thought of as a Japanese phenomenon resulting from social features unique to Japanese culture. However, it has now been recognized that the core features that lead to
55 people withdrawing from society, specifically high social pressure to succeed combined with high youth unemployment and poor youth

Many people think of young Japanese men when they think of hikikomori, but anybody can suffer from social withdrawal.

employment prospects, are not unique to Japan but simply happened in Japan
60 first. Consequently, many countries, including Australia, Brazil, Canada, China, France, India, South Korea, Spain, Thailand, and the United States, have begun reporting cases of hikikomori among their citizens. Furthermore, research indicates that the frequency of hikikomori in those countries is the same as in Japan, at about one percent of people aged between 15 and 39.

15 **CD**

65 **6** Simply forcing hikikomori out of their rooms does not help sufferers of hikikomori syndrome. Doing so can be incredibly stressful and some hikikomori may respond violently. Instead, it is important to approach hikikomori with compassion and understanding. As many hikikomori have accompanying mental health problems, these must be diagnosed and treated at the same time.
70 Since 2009, the Japanese government has supported hikikomori centers in many cities and towns. As well as the hikikomori themselves, these centers also support parents of hikikomori. They provide an important first step in helping the hikikomori reconnect with their parents, society, and themselves. Additionally, some private organizations assist hikikomori by providing them with jobs, and
75 volunteer groups aid in rebuilding the hikikomori's sense of self-worth and encourage them to reintegrate into society.

7 Since hikikomori syndrome first occurred in Japan, the rest of the world is watching Japan closely to find the best ways of helping sufferers of hikikomori syndrome. To do so, we must recognize that hikikomori are not lazy or crazy, but 80 are lost. We need to guide them back to society by providing them with the same reassurances that we all sometimes need – the knowledge that we are not failures and that we can make a positive contribution to society.

Notes

get away from ~「～から離れる、逃れる」 soak（n）「入浴」 solitude「孤独、一人の時間」 coin（vt）「（新語など）を造り出す」 form friendships「友情関係を結ぶ」 the Japanese Cabinet Office「内閣府」 Instagrammable lives「インスタ映えのする生活」無料で写真や動画を共有できる SNS（ソーシャル・ネットワーキング・サービス）の Instagram（インスタグラム）に他人の興味をひきつける内容の投稿ができるよう意識した生活。first-rate「一流の」 economic downturn「（景気などの）下降」 anorexia「食欲不振」 self-worth「自尊心、自分の価値を認識すること」

❯ Questions for Understanding

Part 1 *Look at the following statements about the passage. Write T if the statement is True, and F if it is False. Write the number of the paragraph where you find the answer in the parenthesis.*

1) ____ According to the passage, many hikikomori were bullies during their school lives. （ ）

2) ____ It is correct to say that most hikikomori recover as they get older. （ ）

3) ____ One cause of mental illness is the fact that we cannot possibly achieve everything that society expects of us. （ ）

4) ____ It is well-known that hikikomori syndrome is unique to Japanese culture. （ ）

Part 2 *Look at the following questions about the passage. Check the best answer for each.*

1) Which word has the closest meaning to the word "acute" in Paragraph 2 (line 14)?
a. ☐ moderate   b. ☐ reduced   c. ☐ rigorous   d. ☐ severe

2) Which of the following statements about people who become hikikomori is correct?
   a. ☐ They are young men who could not make friends at school.
   b. ☐ They mostly come from poor families with little money.
   c. ☐ They have multiple difficulties beginning in their youth.
   d. ☐ They are mostly young men between the ages of 15 to 39.

3) Which of the following is true about the international nature of hikikomori?
   a. ☐ Hikikomori outside of Japan are generally aged between 40 and 64.
   b. ☐ The proportion of hikikomori in different countries is about the same.
   c. ☐ Because of its unique culture, there are no hikikomori in the United States.
   d. ☐ While not unique to Japan, hikikomori are an Asian phenomenon.

4) Which of the statements below about the treatment of hikikomori is incorrect?
   a. ☐ Hikikomori often have mental health problems which must also be resolved.
   b. ☐ It is sometimes necessary to pressure hikikomori to re-enter society.
   c. ☐ Developing a hikikomori's self-confidence is important.
   d. ☐ Hikikomori need support and help to create social connections.

❯ Summary

① 17 CD

Fill each space with the best word from the list below.

acute	expectations	reintegrate	anxiety	initially	prospects

While we all need some time to ourselves every now and then, for hikikomori a solitary life becomes their whole existence. Hikikomori were 1) _____ thought to be uniquely Japanese, but it is now understood that this is a global problem. When young people are faced with high social 2) _____ but the 3) _____ of meeting them are poor, some people will respond by withdrawing from society. This is not laziness, however, but a(n) 4) _____ response to the pressures of society that create an unbearable 5) _____ . If we want to encourage hikikomori to 6) _____ into society, we must provide the support and encouragement they need.

Over to You

Choose ONE of the statements below. Prepare a short response giving your opinion.

- **How can we prevent people withdrawing from society?**
- **Hikikomori are just weak.**

....

....

....

....

Not Just for Fun

The Importance of Play and Games

❯ Useful Words

Choose a word from the list below to complete each sentence.

1. Enjoying spending time with friends and family is good for our _____.

2. Eating a balanced diet is _____ to staying healthy.

3. Many chefs use herbs to _____ the flavor of their dishes.

4. To be a good chess player, you need to be able to use a range of different _____.

5. The _____ between the main characters was the best part of the movie.

| interaction | integral | well-being | tactics | enhance |

❯ Reading

① 18~25 CD

18 CD

1 Everyone has played games at some point in their life. Whether they are board games, word games, or card games, people are attracted to them because they are enjoyable and a good way to occupy their time. However, play is more than just fun. In fact, play is so important that the UN Human Rights Office has recognized it as a
10 right of every child. Play is essential to

Playing games together can help families communicate.

human development because it contributes to our physical, mental, social, and emotional well-being. Despite this, opportunities to play have been affected due to our modern lifestyles and changes in family structure. Also, government initiatives, such as the US No Child Left Behind Act of 2001, have increased
15 emphasis on academic study rather than play and being creative. In view of this, it is worthwhile looking at some of the benefits we can get from play.

2 In terms of physical benefits, play provides people with the chance to be active. For children, playing
20 games allows them to practice different physical movements and to test their limits. For adults, it is an opportunity to get away from the constraints of their work desks. In contrast to passive
25 entertainment, active play helps people build strong, healthy bodies.

19 CD

Active play helps keep our bodies strong and healthy.

Furthermore, as play increases our physical activity levels, it is often cited as an essential strategy in the fight against the rise of obesity.

20 CD

3 Play is also integral to mental development. Research has shown that
30 children who play regularly can adapt to different situations more easily. This can enhance their abilities to learn and solve problems. By playing games, we can learn not only strategy and how to win, but also how to apply that knowledge to other parts of our lives. In some education systems, problem-solving games are used to reinforce the theories that are being taught, and the
35 results have generally been excellent.

21 CD

4 However, the mental benefits of play and games are not only developmental, but also preventative. As many people have begun to focus more on work and other commitments, they have less time for fun. This can lead to a build-up of stress and other mental issues such as anxiety. Play can add joy to
40 our lives and relieve stress. Furthermore, concentrating and paying attention to details such as rules, your opponent, and tactics keeps people engaged and mentally active. This is significant in old age as it can help protect us against dementia, including Alzheimer's disease.

22 CD

5 There are also a large number of social benefits that can be gained from
45 play. During childhood, play helps develop and improve social skills. Children
learn about verbal communication, body language, cooperation, negotiation,
and teamwork. As adults, we can continue to refine these skills through play.
Playing games together is one of the most effective ways of starting a friendship
with someone and also maintaining that relationship. Through regular play, we
50 learn to trust one another and feel safe. Play can also help us to resolve conflict
and avoid resentment.

23 CD

6 The interaction experienced during play is also vital in developing social
understanding between children and adults. When parents play with their
children or watch them playing with their friends, they can begin to see the
55 world from their children's perspective. This can help parents to communicate
more effectively with their children. Furthermore, children with less developed
verbal skills may be more comfortable expressing their views, experiences, and
even frustrations through play, due to a sense of distancing themselves from any
negative outcomes. This allows their parents an opportunity to understand them
60 better. Also, actively playing together shows children that their parents are fully
paying attention to them, which helps to strengthen their relationships.

24 CD

7 As well as being fun, play allows children the chance to create and
explore the world in a safe environment. They can practice adult roles, which can
reduce their anxiety when entering society as adults in the future. Additionally,
65 the mental stimulation that play provides can help to build confidence. Finally,
when play is directed by the children themselves, they can discover their own
areas of interest. This will help them find their passions and future goals.

25 CD

8 Play is an essential part of childhood that helps children develop and
allows parents the opportunity to fully engage with their children. However, a
70 number of factors are impacting on the amount of time spent actively playing. It
is important for people to find a balance in their lives between work, study, and
play. Doing so helps us to stay healthy, and it is also fun. Incorporating more fun
and play into your daily life can improve the quality of your relationships, as
well as your mood and outlook. Even in the most difficult of times, taking time
75 away from troubles to play can make us feel better. The good feeling that comes

from having fun while playing remains with us even after the game itself has finished. This makes it easier to maintain a positive and optimistic attitude through difficult situations. So, try to make time to play, it could be the best thing you ever do for yourself.

Notes

game「遊戯、遊び」かくれんぼや鬼ごっこなどルールのある遊びのこと。**word game**「言葉遊び」綴り替えなどを含めた語句に関する遊び。**the UN Human Rights Office**（= **Office of the United Nations High Commissioner for Human Rights**）「国際連合人権高等弁務官事務所」**government initiatives**「政府の新政策」**the US No Child Left Behind Act**「アメリカ落ちこぼれ防止法」初等中等学校制度の改善と授業についていけない生徒をなくすことを目指した政策。2014年までに全生徒が英語と数学において習熟レベルに達することを目標とした。**worthwhile**「価値のある、やりがいのある」**constraint**「拘束」**obesity**「肥満」**preventative**（= **preventive**）「予防的な、防止に役立つ」**commitment**「しなくてはならないこと」**build-up**「増加、蓄積」**dementia**「認知症」**Alzheimer's disease**「アルツハイマー病」**resentment**「憤り、恨み」**engage with ~**「～とふれ合う、関わり合う」

❯ Questions for Understanding

Part 1　*Look at the following statements about the passage. Write T if the statement is True, and F if it is False. Write the number of the paragraph where you find the answer in the parenthesis.*

1) ＿＿＿ Passive entertainment helps people build strong, healthy bodies.　（　）

2) ＿＿＿ Playing with people can help build trust.　（　）

3) ＿＿＿ Play can help parents communicate better with their children.　（　）

4) ＿＿＿ Play helps children find their passions and future goals.　（　）

Part 2　*Look at the following questions about the passage. Check the best answer for each.*

1) Play is essential to human development because it contributes to our ＿＿＿＿＿＿＿ well-being.
a. ☐ physical
b. ☐ mental
c. ☐ emotional
d. ☐ physical, mental, and emotional

2) What are used in some education systems to reinforce theories?
a. ☐ Different situations
b. ☐ Strategies of how to win
c. ☐ Problem solving games
d. ☐ Excellent results

3) How can concentrating and paying attention to details benefit us?
a. ☐ By keeping people engaged and mentally active
b. ☐ By helping people focus more on work and other commitments
c. ☐ By reducing stress and other mental issues
d. ☐ By reducing anxiety

4) Which word has the closest meaning to the word "engage" in Paragraph 8 (line 69)?
a. ☐ communicate
b. ☐ use
c. ☐ involve
d. ☐ attract

❯ Summary

① 26 CD

Fill each space with the best word from the list below.

among	development	introduction
acknowledge	encourage	identified

While the importance of exercise and rest to our health is well-recognized, people often do not **1)** _____ just how essential play is to our well-being. However, the benefits are numerous and wide-ranging. At schools, colleges, and universities, the **2)** _____ of games can help students consolidate knowledge and understanding. In our personal lives, play can aid the **3)** _____ of relationships. This is of particular importance in families. Advantages of play can also be **4)** _____ at workplaces, too, with increased productivity and a greater feeling of togetherness **5)** _____ employees. As a result, some companies **6)** _____ employees to play games such as table tennis or table football together.

❯ Over to You

Choose ONE of the statements below. Prepare a short response giving your opinion.

- **Japanese parents should play more with their children.**
- **Play is the most important activity children can do at kindergarten.**

....

....

....

....

Chapter 4

See It While You Can

The Risks of Over-Tourism

❯ Useful Words

Choose a word from the list below to complete each sentence.

1. Tokyo has over 9 million _____ .

2. One of the _____ of some medicines is that they can make people sleepy or drowsy.

3. In order to _____ people from smoking, health warnings are put on tobacco products in many countries.

4. The old concert hall was _____ and a new building was put up in its place.

5. In 2013, Mount Fuji was _____ as a World Heritage Site.

deter	designated	downsides	demolished	inhabitants

❯ Reading

① 27~33

27

1 Close your eyes and think of a beach. The sand is golden, the sea is clean, and the air is refreshing. For many, that would be an ideal place to live near. Now imagine that same beach, but with 10,000 tourists on it. That image does not seem so appealing.

28

5 **2** Tourism can provide an incredible economic boost to an area and its inhabitants. It is also good for people to travel the world and explore its beauty. However, a downside of this is over-tourism, which is when too many tourists visit a destination. Few places around the world are able to welcome large

numbers of tourists and avoid the negative impacts of over-tourism. In an
10 attempt to counter some of the issues, many destinations have introduced new
rules and regulations.

3 Once better known as Ayers Rock, Uluru in Australia attracts more than 300,000 visitors every year. Before
15 October 2019, visitors were allowed to climb Uluru. However, Uluru is sacred to the indigenous Anangu people. Despite this, tourists were leaving trash and vandalizing the culturally
20 significant ancient rock paintings and engravings. Furthermore, the climb was often dangerous and temperatures

Visitors are now prohibited from climbing Uluru.

peak at 47C during the hottest months. Since the 1950s, dozens of people have
died on Uluru due to accidents and dehydration, including a Japanese tourist in
25 2018. In 2017, the board members of the Uluru-Kata Tjuta National Park voted
unanimously to prohibit the climb. As the ban approached, the number of
tourists increased. Local accommodation became fully booked, leading to
tourists camping illegally and dumping waste. Now the ban has been
implemented, it is hoped the damage caused by tourists will stop.

30 🎧

30   4 In 2018, 10 million travelers visited Mallorca, the largest of Spain's
Balearic Islands, which is famed for its beaches. That was up from 6 million in
2010. During the peak season, which runs from May through October, more than
1,000 flights land on the island every day. Arrivals by sea are also very high, with
as many as 17,000 cruise ship passengers arriving on some days. All of these
35 arrivals negatively affect the island and its inhabitants due to overcrowding and
air and noise pollution. To raise awareness of these impacts, local groups
distribute fliers in Catalan, English, and German to tourists, highlighting the
environmental problems on the island. As well as the work of these groups, local
officials announced a doubling of the tourist tax to €4 per person per day in
40 2010. Visitors pay the tax when checking out of hotels. It is claimed the funds
will not only deter tourists from visiting but will also be used to try to reverse
some of the damage already done.

31 CD

Many beaches can become overcrowded, like Bondi Beach in Australia.

5   Boracay is a beautiful island in the Philippines with an area of just six square kilometers. Due to that beauty, the number of annual visitors soared from 260,000 in 2000 to more than two million in 2018. While those in the tourism industry profited, many issues such as waste and trash management worsened. Consequently, the once-clear waters became polluted, and illegal fishing and unmonitored snorkeling destroyed 70-90 percent of the coral reefs. To combat this, in February 2018, Philippine President Rodrigo Duterte demanded a six-month closure to tourists. Properties built on the beaches illegally were demolished, and all hotels were forced to apply for a new set of permits with stricter regulations. There are further plans to limit the number of travelers and workers on the island. The island reopened to tourists in October 2018, but the government is continuing to carefully monitor the situation.

32 CD

6   Located around 950 kilometers off the coast of Ecuador, the 19 islands that make up the Galápagos host approximately 9,000 unique species, both on land and in their surrounding waters. However, any changes to the environment in the area threaten the survival of those species. A large increase in cruises to the Galápagos not only fueled immigration, but also damaged the animals' natural habitats and led to the introduction of invasive species. As a result, the United Nations listed the destination as an endangered heritage site. Following the UN listing, significant changes to cruise travel regulations were made. This led to ship-based tourism decreasing by 11 percent from 2007 to 2016. However, overall visitors increased by 39 percent, with land-based tours rising 90 percent during that time. Consequently, 97 percent of the land area has been designated as part of a protected national park. Tourism is also being restricted, with visitors only able to go to specific visitor sites and only when accompanied by a licensed Galápagos National Park Guide.

33 CD

7   The world's population is increasing, and more people are traveling abroad every year. With so much demand, it is important for travelers to be mindful of how and when they travel. This does not always happen, so new rules and restrictions have been introduced. However, with so many stakeholders involved and so much money to be made, any changes are met with resistance. 80 Despite this, protecting our world's most beautiful and interesting destinations must be a priority so that future generations can also enjoy visiting them.

Notes

Ayers Rock「エアーズロック」オーストラリアの準州 Northern Territory（ノーザンテリトリー）にある岩山。先住民の聖地で彼らが呼ぶ Uluru（ウルル）が正式名称。**Anangu people**「アナング、オーストラリア（特に中部の）先住民」**vandalize**「（芸術作品・公共物など）を故意に破壊する」**dehydration**「脱水（症状）」**the Uluru-Kata Tjuta National Park**「ウルル・カタジュタ国立公園」**unanimously**「満場一致で」**Mallorca**「マリョルカ、マジョルカ（島）」**Balearic Islands**「バレアレス諸島」スペインの東岸沖合にあり、地中海西部に位置する島群。中心都市はパルマ。**Catalan**「カタロニア語」スペインのカタロニア地方で使用されている言語。**Boracay**「ボラカイ島」**soar**「急増する」**Rodrigo Duterte**「ロドリゴ・ドゥテルテ（1945-）」**Ecuador**「エクアドル」**The Galápagos**「ガラパゴス」ガラパゴス諸島には特異な動植物が生息し、ダーウィンの進化論に影響を与えた。**fuel**「助長する、あおる」**Galápagos National Park Guide**「ガラパゴス国立公園案内人」**stakeholder**「利害関係者」

❯ Questions for Understanding

Part 1 *Look at the following statements about the passage. Write T if the statement is True, and F if it is False. Write the number of the paragraph where you find the answer in the parenthesis.*

1) _____ From 2010 to 2018, the number of visitors to Mallorca decreased.　（　　）

2) _____ All of the coral reefs on Boracay have been destroyed.　（　　）

3) _____ Changes to the environment in the Galápagos threaten the survival of the species that live there.　（　　）

4) _____ New rules and restrictions are always welcomed when they are introduced.

（　　）

Part 2 *Look at the following questions about the passage. Check the best answer for each.*

1) What did some people use to call Uluru?
　a. ☐ Ayers Rock
　b. ☐ Australia
　c. ☐ Anangu
　d. ☐ The Uluru-Kata Tjuta National Park

2) Which word has the closest meaning to the word "prohibit" in Paragraph 3 (line 26)?
  a. ☐ change
  b. ☐ forbid
  c. ☐ allow
  d. ☐ approve

3) What change is planned in the future on Boracay?
  a. ☐ A six-month closure to tourists
  b. ☐ The demolishing of illegally built properties on the beaches
  c. ☐ The introduction of a new set of permits for hotels
  d. ☐ A limit on the number of travelers and workers on the island

4) By how much did ship-based tourism drop between 2007 and 2016 in the Galápagos?
  a. ☐ 11 percent
  b. ☐ 39 percent
  c. ☐ 90 percent
  d. ☐ 97 percent

❯ Summary

① 34 CD

Fill each space with the best word from the list below.

employment	consequences	imperative
permanently	routines	excessive

Everybody enjoys a good vacation, whether that means traveling abroad or just resting at home. However, there are serious 1) _____ of large numbers of people traveling to different countries. The positives brought by tourism can help an area's economy and improve 2) _____ rates. The negatives can include pollution, damage to natural habitats, 3) _____ noise, and strain being placed on infrastructure. While taking time off and changing our daily 4) _____ can greatly improve our personal well-being, it is 5) _____ that we consider the impact our actions are having on our world. If we do not do that, we could damage our planet 6) _____.

Over to You

Choose ONE of the statements below. Prepare a short response giving your opinion.

- **It is better to travel in our own countries than abroad.**
- **We cannot truly understand a country's culture without visiting that country.**

....

....

....

....

The World's Greatest Gamers

The Rise of Esports

❯ Useful Words

Choose a word or phrase from the list below to complete each sentence.

1. A café in a busy street will usually have a higher _____ than one in a quiet street.

2. Climbing Mount Everest was my greatest _____.

3. Please complete the survey _____; do not tell anyone your answers.

4. Because he overslept, he did not arrive _____ the start of the test.

5. His poor driving skills meant he was a _____ to the other drivers.

| in time for | endeavor | hazard | individually | revenue |

❯ Reading

① 35~40

35

1 Do you enjoy playing video games? Are you good at them? How would you like to play professionally? With estimated audiences of more than 450 million people and revenues of more than $1 billion in 2019, esports have become a global phenomenon. But how did esports begin, and what does it
5 mean to be a professional player of video games?

36

2 The first computer games were developed in the 1950s, not long after the first computers were invented. However, the first truly popular computer game, *Spacewar*, was created in 1962 at the Massachusetts Institute of Technology in the US. In 1972, the first esports tournament took place at Harvard University, with
10 students competing against each other to win games of *Spacewar*. As video arcade

31

games such as *Space Invaders* became popular during the 1970s and 1980s, regular tournaments began to be held. These tournaments could be surprisingly large. The Atari Space Invaders Championship in 1980 had 10,000 competitors, for example. However, these tournaments tended to involve people playing
15 games individually with the winner being the person with the highest score. With the development of publicly available broadband internet services and online games during the 1990s and 2000s, it became possible for individuals and teams to directly compete against each other while spectators watched. In 2000, the South Korean government founded the Korean eSports Association
20 and the modern era of esports was born.

37

3 From 2000 to 2016, the number of esports tournaments rose from 10 to more than 250. The number of people watching esports
25 also grew, with people viewing contests online on streaming services such as Amazon-owned Twitch, and on television channels such as ESPN, a sports channel owned by Disney. At
30 the same time, the prizes for winning esports tournaments also got larger. In

The 2016 League of Legends final was held in the Staples Center in Los Angeles.

1972, the winner of the *Spacewar* tournament received a one-year subscription to *Rolling Stone* magazine. By 2011, the prize pool of just one tournament, The International, was $1.6 million, with a grand prize of $1 million. In the 2019
35 tournament, held in the 18,000-seater Mercedes-Benz Arena in Shanghai, the prize pool was more than $34 million. In 2019, the top-earning American esports player, 16-year-old Kyle Giersdorf, won $3 million playing in a single tournament.

38

4 In order to be able to win tournaments, professional esports players
40 must train surprisingly hard. In 2016, Finnish researchers investigated the kind of training necessary to be an elite esports player. They found that the average professional esports player trained for nearly five and a half hours a day. In fact, practicing more than 50 hours a week is common in many professional teams. Furthermore, at least one hour of that training was physical training. Some

⁴⁵ professional teams provide both gym and game coaches, as well as professional nutritionists to ensure that the players are eating a balanced diet. This amount of training is about ⁵⁰ the same as athletes that compete in the Olympic Games, who generally do five to six hours of training per day. This should not be surprising: achieving an elite level of skill in any ⁵⁵ endeavor requires dedication, discipline, and both mental and physical fitness.

You have to train hard every day if you want to be a professional esports player.

39 CD

5 Like all professional sports, esports have a dark side. As in other sports, injury is a constant danger. Esports players risk career-ending physical problems such as back strain, deep vein thrombosis, and carpal tunnel syndrome. In addition, with prizes worth $1 million there is always the temptation to cheat. ⁶⁰ During the 2012 Major League Gaming Summer Championship, two teams were blocked from receiving their prize money because they had colluded and decided who was going to win before they played. Some players also take drugs to improve their concentration or to help them remain calm during the stress of an intense game. A hazard that is perhaps unique to esports is cancellation. If the ⁶⁵ game maker stops making the game, the professional players' careers can come to a sudden end, as happened in 2018, when the games company Blizzard cancelled the tournaments for its *Heroes of the Storm* game. Finally, while top players can earn millions of dollars a year, many professional esports players earn very little, and may not get paid at all. Since 2015, however, it has become ⁷⁰ more common for professional teams to pay their players a salary. This is important because the career of a professional esports player is not a long one, usually lasting only a few years between the ages of 15 and 25.

40 CD

6 What is the future of esports? Almost certainly, esports will continue to grow in popularity and become a regular part of our sporting experiences. It also ⁷⁵ seems likely that esports will become an Olympic event in the future. However, the era of purely human esports teams may already be coming to an end. Recent developments in artificial intelligence mean that computers can beat humans in even some of the most complex games. Perhaps in a few years we will all be

tuning in to watch human and computer teams compete together to win
⁸⁰ Olympic gold.

Notes

....

Spacewar 「スペースウォー」世界初のシューティングゲーム **The Massachusetts Institute of Technology**
「マサチューセッツ工科大学（**MIT**）」米マサチューセッツ州ケンブリッジにある私立大学。1865 年開校。
Harvard University 「ハーバード大学」米マサチューセッツ州ケンブリッジにある米国最古の大学。1836 年創
立。**video arcade games** 「ビデオアーケードゲーム」コンピューター機能を用いたコイン式のゲーム機。ゲー
ムセンターや娯楽施設などに設置されている。***Space Invaders*** 「スペースインベーダー」(株)タイトーが 1978 年
に発売したゲーム。世界中で人気を博した。**The Atari Space Invaders Championship** 「アタリスペースイン
ベーダー選手権」アタリ社はアメリカのビデオゲーム会社。1972 年創業。**broadband internet service** 「ブ
ロードバンドインターネットサービス」高速度・大容量の情報を送受信できるインターネット接続を用いたサービ
ス。**Korean eSports Association** 「韓国 e スポーツ協会」**streaming service** 「ストリーミングサービス」イン
ターネットでデータ受信と同時に再生を行うことのできるサービス。**Twitch** 「ツイッチ」アマゾン（米のウェ
ブ通販サービス）が提供するゲーム専門のライブ配信サイト。**ESPN** 米国のスポーツ専門チャンネル。1978 年
開設。***Rolling Stone*** 『ローリングストーン』米国の音楽雑誌。1967 年創刊。**a grand prize** 「大賞」**Mercedes-
Benz Arena** 「メルセデスベンツアリーナ」2010 年の上海万博開催時に建造され、現在は複合施設として利用さ
れている。**a balanced diet** 「栄養バランスのとれた食事」**back strain** 「腰椎捻挫」ぎっくり腰。**deep vein
thrombosis** 「深部静脈血栓症」俗にエコノミークラス症候群とも言う。**carpal tunnel syndrome** 「手根管症候
群」**Blizzard** 「ブリザード」米国のゲーム会社。***Heroes of the Storm*** ブリザード社が開発したオンラインゲー
ム。2015 年サービス開始。

▶ Questions for Understanding

Part 1 *Look at the following statements about the passage. Write T if
the statement is True, and F if it is False. Write the number of the
paragraph where you find the answer in the parenthesis.*

1) ____ According to the passage, there have been esports tournaments for around
50 years. ( )

2) ____ The development of the internet was essential for modern esports. ( )

3) ____ Although originally American, esports are now played only in South Korea.

( )

4) ____ Despite their popularity, there is little chance that esports will be seen at the
Olympic Games. ( )

Part 2 *Look at the following questions about the passage. Check the
best answer for each.*

1) Where was the world's first esports tournament held?
    a. ☐ Shanghai   b. ☐ South Korea
    c. ☐ The Massachusetts Institute of Technology   d. ☐ Harvard University

2) Which of the following is correct about professional esports players?
- a. ☐ They usually train for nearly five and a half hours a week.
- b. ☐ They can easily earn more than $1 million in a year.
- c. ☐ They do a lot of physical training as well as playing games.
- d. ☐ They usually end their careers with back strain, deep vein thrombosis, and carpal tunnel syndrome.

3) Which word has the closest meaning to the word "hard" in Paragraph 4 (line 40)?
- a. ☐ difficulty   b. ☐ lazily   c. ☐ intensely   d. ☐ easily

4) What problem may be unique to esports?
- a. ☐ Being forced to stop playing because of physical injury
- b. ☐ Having your sport vanish when a game stops being sold
- c. ☐ Being unable to continue because you do not earn enough money
- d. ☐ Losing a game because another team is cheating

❯ Summary

① 41 CD

Fill each space with the best word from the list below.

spectators	temptation	subscription
dedicated	collude	competitors

Many people are surprised to discover that esports tournaments have been taking place since the early 1970s. However, it is only in recent years that esports have become an international sport with **1)** _____ professional **2)** _____ playing in front of thousands of **3)** _____. The rise in popularity of esports has also meant a rise in the value of prizes that can be won, from a magazine **4)** _____ in 1972 to millions of dollars in 2019. Unfortunately, like many other professional sports, the chance to win a fortune means that players are sometimes faced with the **5)** _____ to cheat, perhaps by trying to **6)** _____ with other players. If esports remain popular it is possible that they will become an Olympic sport someday.

Over to You

Choose ONE of the statements below. Prepare a short response giving your opinion.

- **Esports are not really sports.**
- **Esports should be in the Olympic Games.**

....

....

....

....

Chapter 6

3D-Printed Limbs and Robot Doctors

Amazing Advances in Medicine

❯ Useful Words

Choose a word from the list below to complete each sentence.

1. Because she grew up in a big city, it took her a while to _____ to life in the country.

2. He picked up the cookie and took a bite. Unfortunately, it was _____ and made of plastic.

3. The doctor took a _____ of her blood in order to find out what was wrong with her.

4. I will _____ this house when my grandfather dies.

5. After waiting in line for three hours, he was able to _____ his favorite singer's autograph.

> inherit   artificial   adapt   obtain   specimen

❯ Reading

① 42~48

42

1 Throughout history, people have had accidents and suffered from illnesses. As a result, every culture developed first aid to deal with injuries, and discovered plants that could help people recover from sickness. However, until recently the human body was not well understood, and the causes of most
5 diseases were unknown. This meant that traditional medical treatments sometimes worked, sometimes did nothing, and sometimes made things worse. When scientific approaches began to be applied to medicine during the 19th century, it became possible to better understand the body, the causes of disease,

and how medicines functioned. Consequently, the most effective treatments and medicines from China, Europe, India, and other cultures around the world were combined to create modern medicine.

2 It is sometimes difficult to appreciate how much modern medicine has changed our world. In 1800, the average global life expectancy was 28.5 years. By 1900, this had risen by just a little, to 32 years. By 2000, it was 66.3 years, increasing to 72.6 years in 2019. In some countries, such as Japan, people have average life expectancies of nearly 85 years. Let's look at some of the amazing developments that medical scientists are working on today.

3 *Hero Arms for Hero Kids*. Every year, about 1 million people lose a limb due to disease or injury, and twice as many are born with limb differences, that is arms or legs that have developed in an unusual way. As well as the physical problems that can result from having a missing or anomalous limb, about one third of

This British girl received two Hero Arms.

people with limb differences or amputations also suffer from psychological problems, including depression and anxiety. For children, whose bodies are rapidly growing and changing, body image issues can be a major problem. One reason for this is that the prostheses used to replace their missing limbs may not look good or fit well. To resolve this problem, Open Bionics, a British company, has developed the Hero Arm to provide prosthetic arms that children will be happy owning and using. Each arm is 3D-printed so that it fits its user perfectly. Furthermore, the cover of the arm can be customized with various designs, including several from Disney. Unfortunately, the Hero Arm cannot restore feeling to the users currently, but this technology is also being developed. American company Psyonic has created a prosthetic hand which provides users with feeling in their artificial fingertips, while researchers at the Swiss Federal Institute of Technology have developed prosthetic legs that users can feel, increasing their walking speed by up to six meters a minute.

4 *The Robot Will See You Now*. Children can often adapt to new situations

and technology far faster than adults can. Since 2016, children attending kindergarten in China have had health checks every morning. In more than 2,000 Chinese preschools, these daily health checks are conducted by Walklake,
45 a friendly robot. A three-second greeting to Walklake allows the robot to detect if the student has a fever, blisters on their hands, a sore throat, or red eyes. If the robot finds any of these symptoms, it contacts the school nurse, who checks the student again and decides what action to take. Finally, after checking all of the students, Walklake sends a report to the school principal.

46 **CD**

50 **5** *AI Can Do It.* As well as controlling health-checking robots, artificial intelligence is also being used in hospitals. Many health problems such as some kinds of cancers can be treated easily if they are detected quickly. The
55 problem for doctors is that detecting these problems requires looking at specimens containing thousands of cells in order to identify small changes in some of them. To do this well

Is this the future of medicine?

needs a lot of training. It is also time-consuming as each sample must be
60 checked by two doctors in order to avoid errors. However, an AI system can perform these checks much faster and, since it does not get tired, makes fewer errors. Even so, AI systems are not perfect, and it has been found that the best results are obtained when a doctor and an AI system work together.

47 **CD**

6 *Make Me a Baby.* Screening programs can rapidly identify health
65 problems, but surely it would be better to avoid them altogether. Recent developments in genetics, such as the CRISPR tool, mean that it may soon be possible to modify human DNA in order to prevent people from developing certain diseases or illnesses. This may be especially effective for inherited conditions. For example, some people from Siberia have an unusual form of the
70 GJB2 gene. As a result, children who have two versions of this gene cannot hear. Scientists in Russia are planning to modify the GJB2 gene in volunteers from Siberia so that their children will be able to hear normally.

48 **CD**

7 The potential of these new medical technologies is huge. However, when introducing them, we must be careful not to rely on technology at the expense of human knowledge and skill. Furthermore, now that we have the technology to modify our own DNA, we must ensure that there are good ethical reasons for doing so. If we can meet these challenges, we can be confident that medical research will continue to bring us ever longer and healthier lives.

Notes

first aid「救急処置」**limb difference**「肢障害」**anomalous**「形態異常の」**amputation**「(外科手術による)切断」**prostheses**「義肢」**prosthesis** の複数形 **Open Bionics**「オープンバイオニクス社」3D プリントによる義手を製造販売する英国企業。2014 年設立。**Hero Arm**「ヒーローアーム」オープンバイオニクス社による節電義手(筋肉が発する電気信号を読み取り、動かすことができる義手)。アニメやゲームなどのキャラクターデザインを取り入れている。**Psyonic**「サイオニック社」節電義手を開発製造する米国企業 **the Swiss Federal Institute of Technology**「スイス連邦工科大学」スイス連邦チューリッヒ市にある国立大学。1855 年創立。**Walklake**「ウォークレイク」人工知能を搭載した中国の健康診断ロボット。**blister**「水疱」**genetics**「遺伝学」**the CRISPR tool**「CRISPR ツール」遺伝子編集技術のこと。

▶ Questions for Understanding

Part 1 *Look at the following statements about the passage. Write T if the statement is True, and F if it is False. Write the number of the paragraph where you find the answer in the parenthesis.*

1) ____ According to the passage, people today live half as long as they did in 1800.   (   )

2) ____ About 30 percent of people with anomalous limbs suffer from psychological problems.   (   )

3) ____ If Walklake discovers that a child is sick, it contacts the school principal.   (   )

4) ____ The passage indicates that there may sometimes be good reasons to change our DNA.   (   )

Part 2 *Look at the following questions about the passage. Check the best answer for each.*

1) Which of the following statements about traditional medical treatments is correct?
   a. ☐ Traditional medical treatments were better than modern medicine.
   b. ☐ Traditional medical treatments are popular in China, Europe, and India.
   c. ☐ Traditional medical treatments were not always safe or reliable.
   d. ☐ Traditional medical treatments were invented during the 19th century.

2) Which word has the closest meaning to the word "anomalous" in Paragraph 3 (line 26)?

a. ☐ common   b. ☐ unusual   c. ☐ typical   d. ☐ unexceptional

3) What is the Hero Arm?

a. ☐ It is a prosthesis that its users can feel.
b. ☐ It is a robot arm used by doctors in China.
c. ☐ It is an artificial hand made by Disney.
d. ☐ It is a prosthetic limb designed for young people.

4) According to the passage, what is the best way of using AI in medicine?

a. ☐ Using it to train doctors to do medical checks faster and with fewer errors
b. ☐ Using it together with a doctor in order to maximise effectiveness
c. ☐ Using it to develop robot doctors that can conduct health checks
d. ☐ Using it to accurately modify human DNA to prevent inherited conditions

❯ Summary

① 49

Fill each space with the best word or phrase from the list below.

| limbs | conduct | modify | currently | expectancy | rely on |

In the past 200 years, medical research has more than doubled our average life 1) _____. Medical technologies that are 2) _____ being developed include improved prosthetic 3) _____ that function in more natural ways and medical robots that can 4) _____ health checks and even detect if someone has a fever. Artificial intelligence systems are working together with human doctors in order to speed up the analysis of medical specimens and rapidly identify health problems. We can even 5) _____ our genetic code so that children can avoid inheriting the health problems of their parents and grandparents. These technologies are very powerful, however, and we must be certain that there are good ethical reasons for using them before we begin to 6) _____ them.

Over to You

Choose ONE of the statements below. Prepare a short response giving your opinion.

- **People should be allowed to design their own children.**
- **I would not trust a robot doctor.**

....

....

....

....

Chapter 7

Fake Burgers and Electric Gum

The Future of Food

Useful Words

Choose a word or phrase from the list below to complete each sentence.

1. Many people are surprised to learn that the Hawaiian pizza is part of Canadian _____.

2. Our regular teacher was sick, so today we were taught by a(n) _____ teacher.

3. Many workers lost their jobs and needed government _____ during the Covid-19 pandemic.

4. Because of her poor performance at work she is _____ being fired.

5. Some people like to _____ the clothes they buy in order to create their own style.

> modify   aid   cuisine   substitute   at risk of

Reading

① 50~56

50 🖸

1 In 2019, about 11.5 percent of the world's land was used for growing crops and another 38.5 percent was used for raising animals. Despite using half of the land in the world to produce food, nearly 30 percent of the global population does not have enough to eat. Furthermore, 70 percent of the ocean's
5 fisheries were at risk of overfishing or were already overfished. Combined with a growing world population and the challenges that climate change is bringing, how we eat and what we eat will have to change in the future. Let's consider some of the possibilities.

2 *Bug Brunch:* One option is to get our protein and fats from insects. This should not be so surprising as many cultures include insects in their traditional cuisine, such as the Japanese dish *inago no tsukudani.* Farming insects requires far fewer resources than farming animals and produces much less waste. Additionally, insects can be fed on food waste. Globally, nearly one third

Eating insects is a tradition in many cultures. In Thailand, people often buy insects as snacks from street-side stalls.

of all food produced is wasted every year. In Japan, that represents 6.5 million tons of lost food. As some people find the idea of eating insects to be unpleasant, the first step is using insect protein and fats to replace the use of fish and soy in animal feed. This could have a big impact on the environment because a quarter of the fish we catch, and 80 percent of the soy we grow, are used to feed the animals we eat.

3 *Fake Burgers:* If bingeing on bugs does not appeal to you, then perhaps you would prefer to eat a fake burger instead. One barrier to encouraging people to eat less meat is that meat replacements simply do not taste good enough. However, that has started to change, with companies such as Impossible Foods producing vegetarian products that look, smell, and taste like the meat they are replacing. But are these meat substitutes really any good? In June 2019, New Zealand pizza chain Hell Pizza added a special Burger Pizza to its menu for one day. It was quite a popular choice, and around 3,000 were sold. The Burger Pizza was completely meat free, but none of the customers noticed. Hell Pizza is not the only fast food chain to begin selling meat-free products. In 2019, KFC began selling vegetarian nuggets and wings at some US stores, Burger King introduced its Impossible Whopper, and McDonald's created the PLT, or Plant, Lettuce, Tomato burger. These meat-free replacements will likely become a common sight on fast-food menus around the world.

4 *Fresh from the Lab:* Another alternative to farming animals for meat is cultured meat. Like farming insects, growing meat in a laboratory requires far

less land and resources than raising animals. Furthermore, no animals have to die. The first burger made from
45 cultured meat was cooked in 2013. Today, many companies, including Japan's Nissin Food Holdings, are trying to produce cultured meat and fish. However, cultured meat is

Would you eat meat grown in a laboratory?

50 currently too expensive to be commercially successful. The Japanese company IntegriCulture, working with JAXA and Tokyo Women's Medical University, has managed to reduce the cost of their cultured meat to less than $200 per kilogram. While this is much less than the $250,000 the first cultured burger cost, it is still a long way from the $2 per kilogram cost necessary for cultured
55 meat to be an economically viable product.

54 CD

5 *Superfoods:* The changing climate means that our food crops and animals will need to adapt to hotter temperatures and other environmental challenges, including new diseases. Traditionally, farmers bred the crops and animals which were most successful to produce the varieties that we know today. The problem
60 with the traditional method is that it takes a long time. For example, it took at least 3,000 years to develop the modern tomato. In 2018, scientists in Brazil and China showed that genetic modification (GM) could reduce this time to just three years. Other GM products include apples that never go brown, high-fiber wheat, healthier cooking oils, and rice and bananas that contain vitamin A.
65 Unfortunately, due to public misunderstanding about GM foods, many people fear them, and some countries have banned them. This is frustrating because the processes that scientists use to genetically modify plants and animals are also found in nature. It is now known that some viruses and bacteria can naturally genetically modify plants and animals. For example, in 2019 it was discovered
70 that the genomes of at least 5 percent of plants naturally include DNA from the *Agrobacterium* bacteria, including bananas, tea, yams, cranberries, cherries, and hops.

55 CD

6 *Electric Gum:* Today, nearly 40 percent of the global population is overweight or obese. But perhaps the electric gum invented by scientists at Meiji
75 University in 2018 can help. As it is chewed, the gum uses small amounts of

electricity on the tongue and this causes people to experience different flavors. Artificial food aids like this may help people to control their eating and lose weight.

56 🎧 CD

7 The world is changing, and our diets will have to change in response.
80 Developments such as cultured meat, GM crops, eating insects, and artificial foods can help us to both eat more healthily and to reduce our impact on the global environment.

Notes
....

overfishing「（魚の）乱獲」**binge**「むやみに食べる」**Impossible Foods**「インポッシブルフーズ」植物由来の代替肉食品を開発・製造している米国企業。2011 年設立。**cultured meat**「培養肉」**IntegriCulture**「（株）インテグリカルチャー」化粧品、食品、細胞培養肉の研究開発を行う日本企業。2015 年設立。**JAXA**「日本宇宙航空研究開発機構」**viable**「採算の取れる」**genetic modification**「遺伝子組み換え」**high-fiber**「（食品が）高繊維質の、植物繊維を多く含む」**genome**「ゲノム」細胞の中にある一組の染色体およびその全遺伝情報。**Agrobacterium**「アグロバクテリウム」**obese**（**adj.**）「肥満の」

❯ Questions for Understanding

Part 1 *Look at the following statements about the passage. Write T if the statement is True, and F if it is False. Write the number of the paragraph where you find the answer in the parenthesis.*

1) ____ According to the passage, about one third of the world's land is dedicated to farming. （   ）

2) ____ One reason to farm insects is that they can eat the food we throw away. （   ）

3) ____ New Zealand pizza chain Hell Pizza provided free meat products for one day in June 2019. （   ）

4) ____ In 2019, scientists genetically modified more than 5 percent of plants. （   ）

Part 2 *Look at the following questions about the passage. Check the best answer for each.*

1) According to the passage, why might insect protein be used in animal feed?
  a. ☐ Because 25 percent of the fish we catch are used in animal feed.
  b. ☐ Because people waste one third of the food that is produced every year.
  c. ☐ Because consuming insects is not a pleasant idea for some people.
  d. ☐ Because four fifths of the soy we grow is used in animal feed.

2) What is the main problem with cultured meat and fish?
   a. ☐ The cost to produce it is too high.
   b. ☐ It is too similar to farming insects.
   c. ☐ It requires more resources than raising animals.
   d. ☐ It does not require the death of any animals.

3) Which word has the closest meaning to the word "modification" in Paragraph 5 (line 62)?
   a. ☐ repair   b. ☐ difference   c. ☐ stabilization   d. ☐ alteration

4) What did Brazilian and Chinese scientists do in 2018?
   a. ☐ They showed that genetic modification can be more than 99 percent faster than traditional methods.
   b. ☐ They developed a variety of tomato that no one had eaten for more than 3,000 years.
   c. ☐ They created apples that never go brown, high-fiber wheat, healthier cooking oils, and rice and bananas that contain vitamin A.
   d. ☐ They bred the most successful crops and animal varieties that we know of today.

❯ Summary

① 57 **CD**

Fill each space with the best word from the list below.

artificial	obese	alternative	fisheries	cultured	diet

While 40 percent of us are overweight or 1) _____, 30 percent do not get enough food to eat. This is despite our using half of the world's land for agriculture and emptying our 2) _____ of fish. With climate change and an increasing global population threatening our food supply, it is clear that we will have to make changes to our 3) _____ in the future. Getting our protein from insects is one 4) _____ to farming animals. Another is creating 5) _____ meat and fish in laboratories. Genetic modification of crops will also help us prepare for a hotter world. However, a major problem is convincing people that these 6) _____ approaches to producing food are as good as traditional approaches.

Choose ONE of the statements below. Prepare a short response giving your opinion.

- **It would be better for the world if everyone had a vegetarian diet.**
- **I think the genetic modification of the plants and animals we eat is dangerous.**

....

....

....

....

The Sports Space Race

Chapter 8

The Impact of Science in Sports

❯ Useful Words

Choose a word or phrase from the list below to complete each sentence.

1. Before writing an essay, students should spend five minutes thinking about the topic to _____ ideas.

2. The ski instructor put on her skis to _____ the best way of doing it.

3. Jeans are popular all around the world because they are both fashionable and _____.

4. After lots of studying, the student was _____ able to pass the exam.

5. In order to succeed, practice and training are _____.

eventually	demonstrate	vital	come up with	durable

❯ Reading

① 58~66

58 🔊

1 When people think about sports, they normally come up with ideas such as fitness, fun, competition, and health. Two words that would not commonly be thought of are science and technology. At its most basic, sporting activity involves training hard in order to jump higher, run faster, or lift heavier weights.
5 However, when we start to look more closely at how athletes attempt to do that, we realize that science and technology are just as much a part of sports as pushing our bodies to their limits. From creating the perfect amount of bounce in a tennis ball to the sensors that golfers can use to track the efficiency of their swings, science and technology have impacted greatly on the way in which sports
10 are played and watched. The following examples demonstrate how.

2 *A need for speed.* While advances in technology affect almost all sports, possibly the most notable changes have been in cycling. Every
15 part of a bicycle, from the frame to the gears, has been engineered to make sure they are as light, durable, and aerodynamic as possible. One way of achieving this has been using
20 cutting-edge composite materials.

59 CD

Technology has strongly impacted racing bicycle designs.

Manufacturers have moved away from traditional materials, such as steel and aluminum, and now use carbon fiber, which is both very strong and very light.

60 CD

3 *Analyze this.* Analyzing our movements can help us learn how far we can hit a ball, how we can move more efficiently through water, and even why long
25 jumpers travel further when they move their arms in a certain way. Recognizing this, new technology has been developed that enables teams and athletes to upload videos of training sessions, competitions, and matches, and edit them to identify different possible outcomes and scenarios. This can help them improve their technique, form, and tactical awareness. It can also be used to watch how
30 an opposing team plays, too.

61 CD

4 *Get the message.* In sports, communicating with teammates and coaches successfully is hugely important. In 1994, the NFL, the US American football league, decided to allow quarterbacks to use in-helmet headsets to talk with coaches via radio. This allows them to interact with people both on and off the
35 field more easily. In addition, Major League Baseball teams have begun testing watches that connect pitchers to catchers. The watches enable the players to communicate secretly. Why is this important? It prevents other teams from "sign-stealing," something the Houston Astros were accused of in the 2018 playoffs. While that team was eventually found to be not guilty of cheating, the recording
40 of opposing players' signs and gestures is still a controversial topic.

62 CD

5 *Playing it safe.* Technology in sports aids not only performance, but also safety. One of the best examples of this is the introduction of smart helmets in

American football. As player concussions were damaging the image of the sport, technology that is able to both detect and disperse force and heavy impact was built into the new helmets. This decreases the chances of head injury and means medical staff can immediately help players with possible concussions. In other sports, wearable computers allow athletes' pulse rate, hydration, and temperature to be tracked. Since their introduction, incidences of dehydration, heart attacks, and deaths in many sports have been dramatically reduced.

63 CD

6　*Food for thought*. Outside of training, athletes must think about their diets, too. Sports dietitians and nutritionists use a range of strategies to boost performance, strictly managing not only calorie intake, but also levels of macro- and micro-nutrients. Scientists have even developed indigestible pills that can be used to observe body temperature accurately. The pills move around the gastrointestinal tract and transmit vital information about the body to medical personnel. It is claimed that they will help to minimize deaths from heat exhaustion, which is the second most common reason for athlete fatalities.

64 CD

7　*The show must go on*. The experience of attending a live sporting event nowadays is very different from in the past. Whereas previously, games might have been called off or postponed due to bad weather, now many stadiums have domes. Underground heating also means that the pitches never freeze. However, the cold is not the only problem being faced. In Japan, organizers of the 2020 Olympics trialed a snow machine that was used to blow around 300kg of snow onto spectators at a canoeing event. They did this to help them avoid overheating and suffering from sunstroke.

65 CD

8　*A level playing field*. Science has also played a huge role in supporting athletes with disabilities. In the past, people with disabilities often did not have the chance to compete. However, the advancement of prosthetic technology has changed that. Researchers at the University of Pittsburgh pioneered the use of body suits fitted with motion sensors that track athletes' movements. After

Advances in prosthetic technology have enabled more athletes to compete.

studying each person's unique movements, custom prosthetics that move more efficiently with their body can be created.

66

9 Some people are born with natural athletic ability. Many sporting stars understand instinctively how to be the best in their field. However, in recent years, technology has had a huge impact on almost every aspect of our lives and sports are no exception. Success in sports does not depend only on technology, and many other factors are at least as important, but it does help us to understand more, achieve more, and appreciate the stars of our favorite sports more.

Notes

aerodynamic「流線型の、空気の抵抗が少ない形の」cutting-edge「最先端の」composite materials「複合材料」carbon fiber「炭素繊維」a long jumper「走り幅跳びの選手」travel「飛ぶ」tactical awareness「戦術的認識」NFL（= National Football League)「全米フットボール連盟」quarterback「クォーターバック」アメフトで攻撃を指揮する選手。the Houston Astros「ヒューストンアストロズ」米国のプロ野球チーム。本拠地はテキサス州ヒューストン。concussion「脳震とう」pulse rate「脈拍数」hydration「水和」体内水分量 dehydration「脱水症状」macro-nutrient「主要栄養素」タンパク質、炭水化物など所要量が多い栄養成分 micro-nutrient「微量栄養素」ビタミンなど少量で足りる栄養成分 indigestible「消化しにくい」 gastrointestinal tract「胃腸管」prosthetic「人工装具の、義肢の」Chapter 6 参照。

❯ Questions for Understanding

Part 1 *Look at the following statements about the passage. Write T if the statement is True, and F if it is False. Write the number of the paragraph where you find the answer in the parenthesis.*

1) _____ People often connect science and technology to sports.　　(　)

2) _____ Moving their arms in a certain way can help long jumpers travel further.

　　　　　　　　　　　　　　　　　　　　　　　　　　　　　　　(　)

3) _____ Major League Baseball teams have been testing in-helmet headsets.

　　　　　　　　　　　　　　　　　　　　　　　　　　　　　　　(　)

4) _____ Nowadays, people with disabilities often do not have the chance to compete.　　　　　　　　　　　　　　　　　　　　　　　　　(　)

Part 2 *Look at the following questions about the passage. Check the best answer for each.*

1) What material do manufacturers use to make bicycles lighter?
   a. ☐ steel
   b. ☐ aluminum
   c. ☐ carbon fiber
   d. ☐ All of the above

2) Which of the following is <u>not</u> listed as something that can be improved from uploading and editing videos?
   a. ☐ technique
   b. ☐ form
   c. ☐ tactical awareness
   d. ☐ other teams

3) Which word has the closest meaning to the word "boost" in Paragraph 6 (line 51)?
   a. ☐ improve
   b. ☐ encourage
   c. ☐ motivate
   d. ☐ manage

4) What is a consequence of underground heating?
   a. ☐ attending events is very different
   b. ☐ games are often called off
   c. ☐ stadiums have domes
   d. ☐ pitches never freeze

❯ Summary

① 67 CD

Fill each space with the best word from the list below.

loyal	increasingly	performances	unfair	greatest	argue

Many people dream of being professional athletes, playing in the

1) _____ stadiums and being supported by thousands of

2) _____ fans. What they do not dream of is the long hours of hard training

and analysis of 3) _____ that sports players do. Technological advances are

making that analysis 4) _____ in-depth and important to achieving success.

While some commentators believe that this is a natural progression, others 5) _____ that access to better technology is giving some athletes in more developed countries a(n) 6) _____ advantage.

⊘ Over to You

Choose ONE of the statements below. Prepare a short response giving your opinion.

- **Sports stars earn too much money.**
- **Students should do more sports lessons at school.**

....

....

....

....

Turn Out the Lights

What Is Light Pollution?

❯ Useful Words

Choose a word from the list below to complete each sentence.

1. Increasing the amount of exercise we do can positively _____ our health.

2. Carbon monoxide is a common air _____.

3. In many countries, _____ between cars are a common form of road accident.

4. Even though lots of people want to try using renewable sources of energy, many of them remain expensive and _____.

5. The researchers decided to _____ a new project investigating the connection between wealth and success.

collisions	affect	undertake	pollutant	inefficient

❯ Reading

① 68~75 CD

68 CD

1 Have you ever looked up at the sky at night and wondered how many stars there are? Throughout history people have used the stars in many
5 different ways, from navigation to telling stories that pass down traditions and culture. Less than 100 years ago, it was usual to see a clear

Nearly 80 percent of North Americans are unable to view the Milky Way.

and starry night sky. Unfortunately, now millions of people around the world are
unable to see the Milky Way, including nearly 80 percent of North Americans.
The reason for this is light pollution, which affects 99 percent of the continental
United States and Europe.

69 CD

2 Most people are aware of the consequences of air, water, and land
pollution, but light is also a pollutant that has numerous negative effects.
Despite not being as immediately noticeable or harmful to public health as other
types of pollution, light pollution has become a major environmental concern,
increasing by approximately two percent a year between 2012 and 2016.
Inappropriate or excessive use of artificial light is not only worsening our view of
the universe, but it is also adversely impacting our environment, our health, and
our energy consumption.

70 CD

3 Wasteful light falling where it is not intended or needed is endangering
ecosystems by harming animals whose life cycles depend on darkness. Many
migratory birds fly at night, using natural light from the stars and the Moon to
help them navigate. These birds become disoriented by the glare of artificial light
over urban areas. The American Bird Conservancy estimates that more than four
million migratory birds die each year following collisions with brightly lit towers
and buildings. In response to this, Canada has passed bird-friendly lighting and
building laws, and now many cities, such as Toronto and New York, participate
in lights-out campaigns during peak migration seasons. However, even outside of
urban areas researchers have identified harmful impacts of light pollution on
species including bats, fish, turtles, and primates.

71 CD

4 For humans, the change between night and day triggers biological cues
that help us maintain regular sleeping patterns. Light pollution interferes with
those cues, and this can affect our health by reducing the production of
melatonin. Low melatonin levels are commonly associated with heart disease,
diabetes, depression, and cancer, particularly breast cancer. Furthermore, Dacher
Keltner, a psychologist at the University of California, claims that the sense of
wonder and awe we feel when looking up at the stars at night can lead to people
displaying better reasoning skills and more kindness.

72 CD

5 A large amount of outdoor lighting used at night is inefficient, with

almost 50 percent of the light coming from streetlamps missing its intended target. As this light is most commonly powered by electricity, it is both
45 damaging to the environment and wastes a lot energy. One way of reducing the energy we waste is by replacing light bulbs with light-emitting diodes (LEDs). When Los

Excessive lighting can have negative effects.

50 Angeles replaced more than 150,000 streetlights with LEDs, the city saved approximately $8 million a year, more than 60 percent of its total lighting costs. Savings of $3 million a year were also reported in San Diego. However, because LEDs are cheaper than light bulbs, they tend to be overused and this increases light pollution.

73 **CD**

55　　**6** As awareness of the dangers of light pollution increases, more action is being taken to reduce artificial light. Simple steps such as closing blinds at night can be adopted by individuals, but other larger projects are also being undertaken. One example is a bicycle path in Lidzbark, Poland, that glows blue in the dark. The asphalt on the path includes synthetic particles, called
60 luminophores, which emit energy captured from sunlight. This energy is used to replace other forms of artificial light, such as streetlamps. Other examples include Dark Sky Parks. These are areas recognized by the International Dark-Sky Association (IDA) that are being protected to preserve their high-quality starry nights. Iriomote-Ishigaki National Park in Okinawa Prefecture is the only Dark-
65 Sky Park in Japan, and one of only three locations of its kind in Asia.

74 **CD**

　　7 In contrast to the attempts to reduce light pollution, there are also other projects being proposed that will add to the amount of light pollution on Earth. In an attempt to reduce street lighting, the city of Chengdu, China, is planning to launch an "illumination satellite" that could be eight times brighter than the
70 moon. It would work by reflecting light from the sun using solar panels. While the satellite could save the city $172 million a year, John Barentine, Director of Public Policy at the IDA, believes it would significantly increase light pollution. In Russia, a company called StartRocket wants to send up to 300 small satellites into Earth's orbit that can be used to display company logos. If this project is

75 successful, people in major cities would be able to look up in the sky and see a commercial instead of the stars.

75 🎧

8 As our production of light increases, our views of the sky are becoming worse. We are harming the environment for other species, our health is being affected, and we are wasting a lot of energy and money. The damaging effects of
80 light pollution will only worsen unless people realize that it can be just as harmful as other types of pollution.

Notes

migratory birds「渡り鳥」 **The American Bird Conservancy**「アメリカ合衆国鳥類保護協会」 **primates**「霊長類の動物」 **biological cues**「生物学的合図」行動や反応を導く感覚信号。**melatonin**「メラトニン」睡眠に作用するホルモン。**diabetes**「糖尿病」 **light-emitting diodes**（**LEDs**）「発光ダイオード」 **Lidzbark**「リズバルク群」 **synthetic particles**「合成粒子」 **luminophores**「発光団」 **Dark Sky Park**「ダークスカイパーク」星空を保護・保存するための取り組みをしている区域。**The International Dark-Sky Association**（**IDA**）「国際ダークスカイ協会」光害を抑え夜間環境の保護を目的とした非営利団体。1988 年設立。**Chengdu**「成都」中国四川省の省都。

❯ Questions for Understanding

Part 1 *Look at the following statements. Write T if the statement is True, and F if it is False. Write the number of the paragraph where you find the answer in the parenthesis.*

1) _____ The majority of people in North America cannot see the Milky Way.

( )

2) _____ The life cycles of some animals depend on darkness. ( )

3) _____ Individuals can help to reduce artificial light pollution. ( )

4) _____ According to the passage, there are three Dark-Sky Parks in Japan.

( )

Part 2 *Look at the questions below. Check the best answer for each.*

1) What do many cities participate in during peak migration seasons?
   a. ☐ Collisions with brightly lit towers
   b. ☐ Bird-friendly lighting and building laws
   c. ☐ Lights-out campaigns
   d. ☐ Research outside of urban areas

2) Which word has the closest meaning to the word "maintain" in Paragraph 4 (line 33)?
   a. ☐ insist
   b. ☐ keep
   c. ☐ allege
   d. ☐ hold

3) Why do light-emitting diodes tend to be overused?
   a. ☐ Their light often misses its intended target.
   b. ☐ They are more common than light bulbs.
   c. ☐ They waste a lot of energy.
   d. ☐ They are cheaper than light bulbs.

4) What could be launched in the city of Chengdu, China?
   a. ☐ An illumination satellite
   b. ☐ The International Dark-Sky Association
   c. ☐ 300 small satellites
   d. ☐ Company logos

❯ Summary

① 76 CD

Fill each space with the best word from the list below.

major	waste	obvious	damaging	natural	huge

Pollution is affecting our lives in many different ways. Plastic bags in oceans are killing marine animals, factories are dumping 1) _____ into rivers which damages the quality of drinking water, and 2) _____ amounts of garbage are being buried underground or burned. Light pollution is also a 3) _____ contributor to the deterioration of the environment. Its effect may not be as 4) _____ as other pollutants, but excessive light is negatively impacting the 5) _____ habitats of a range of urban and rural animals. It is also 6) _____ human health. This is something that we must all think about and try to change.

Choose ONE of the statements below. Prepare a short response giving your opinion.

- **Younger people are more concerned with pollution than older people.**
- **It is the responsibility of governments, not individuals, to reduce pollution.**

....

....

....

....

It's Good to Be Grumpy

The Positive Consequences of Negative Feelings

❯ Useful Words

Choose a word from the list below to complete each sentence.

1. As the tournament progressed, the level of competition _____.

2. All of our actions have _____. We should always try to remember that.

3. Soon after the company was founded, it began to grow and _____.

4. Preparing well for an interview can _____ our chances of getting a job.

5. Children often find singing a _____ way of learning new words and phrases.

> thrive   stimulating   intensified   boost   consequences

❯ Reading

① 77~84 CD

77 CD

1 Many people dream of being a world famous actor. However, is the reality as good as the dream? For people looking at Harrison Ford, for example, they often would not think so. In a career spanning four decades, Ford has starred in movies that have grossed over $9.3 billion worldwide, including
5 blockbusters such as the Star Wars and Indiana Jones series. He has also won the Saturn Award for Best Actor twice (in 1981 and 2016). Despite this, after an interview with GQ magazine in 2012, he was described as the grumpiest man on Earth. While grumpiness is often perceived negatively, has this personality trait
10 helped him to become so successful?

78 CD

2 In recent years, the pursuit of happiness has intensified. Books on how to be happy have become bestsellers, happiness experts can be hired, companies organize self-help courses for their employees, and users on social networking sites gain fame by posting inspirational happiness quotes. Even major institutions are focusing more on happiness. The US army trains its soldiers in positive psychology, and schools in Britain teach optimism classes. But should we really be focusing so much on being happy? After all, good moods can have negative consequences.

79 CD

3 When we are happy, our bodies produce a hormone called oxytocin, which has been shown to reduce our ability to identify threats and dangerous situations. If people are always happy, they tend not to think about or challenge their environment. This means they pay less attention to important details, and thus are more likely to make bad decisions. Additionally, highly positive people can lose motivation and be less creative. Why would you want to change what is making you happy? On the other hand, emotions such as disappointment, fear, anger, and guilt that are often seen as "negative" can lead to advantages. In fact, our negative feelings evolved to serve useful functions and help us thrive.

80 CD

4 One example of this is anger. Many successful people throughout history have had very bad tempers, ranging from scientists like Newton to composers like Beethoven. A more recent example is the founder of Amazon, Jeff Bezos, who built a $300 billion company, despite being known for his angry outbursts. Research is increasingly recognizing that

Can being grumpy help us become successful?

grumpiness and anger can lead to behavior that improves language skills and memory, makes us more persuasive, encourages innovation, and develops problem-solving skills. Furthermore, feeling angry can help us to better understand the people we are angry at and why we are angry.

81 CD

5 But how can anger lead to positive results? When people get angry, adrenaline rushes to the brain, which causes breathing and heart rate to accelerate. This primarily prepares the body for physical aggression. However, if

⁴⁵ people learn to control their aggression, it can boost motivation and assertiveness, and encourage them to take calculated risks. This can have benefits in contexts where competition is important, such as in politics, business, and sport. Furthermore, when we are growing up, controlled aggression is thought to help build autonomy, identity, and engagement with our peers.

⁵⁰   **6** Other "negative" emotions can be advantageous, too. People who show a tendency to feel guilt are often rated as the best leaders on feedback assessments. When we feel fear, our ⁵⁵ ability to focus is heightened, and we become better at blocking out distractions. This enables us to act quickly and discover solutions in dangerous situations. Sadness

82 CD

Can being happy make us less aware of danger?

⁶⁰ makes us pay more attention to details, which helps us understand our surroundings and situations better. This allows us to make better judgements, communicate our feelings better, and construct more persuasive arguments. Being pessimistic can prepare people for different outcomes, which can be stimulating and encourage resourcefulness. Finally, a 2011 study at Tilburg ⁶⁵ University in the Netherlands found that envy led to students performing better in school.

83 CD

7 Even though displaying anger and other "negative" emotions can lead to undesirable results, avoiding them can have more serious consequences. One of the main causes of many psychological problems is known to be the repression ⁷⁰ of unwelcome thoughts or feelings. This may seem surprising because attempting to avoid negative emotions appears to be a natural reaction. Negative emotions often do not feel good, and they are commonly linked to negative events that we want to steer clear of or forget. However, while avoidance can help in the short term, in the long term, it can lead to bigger problems than those we were initially ⁷⁵ trying to get away from. These include depression, health issues, stress, and communication difficulties.

84 CD

8 Given a choice, most people would probably prefer to be happy all the time, and there are obvious advantages to being in a good mood. But it is possible to have too much of a good thing. All emotions are a part of human experience, so should we try to escape from some of them? Can we really experience happiness without sadness, tranquility without anger, and courage without fear? It is important to view traditionally "negative" emotions in terms of their benefits and useful functions. So, if someone tells you to "cheer up," tell them that you are just improving your well-being, productivity, and communication skills by embracing your grumpiness.

Notes

Harrison Ford「ハリソン・フォード (1942-)」米イリノイ州出身の俳優。**blockbuster**「大ヒット作」 **Indiana Jones series**『インディ・ジョーンズ・シリーズ』(日本における名称) 考古学者インディアナ・ジョーンズの冒険を描いた映画シリーズ。1981 年初回作放映。**The Saturn Award for Best Actor**「サターン最優秀主演俳優賞」サターン賞は、映画、テレビなどの優れた SF やファンタジー、ホラー作品に贈られる賞。1972 年創設。**GQ magazine** ファッションやライフスタイルなどの情報を提供する男性向け月刊誌。1931 年創刊。 **oxytocin**「オキシトシン」**Jeff Bezos**「ジェフ・ベゾス (1964-)」米国の実業家・投資家。**adrenaline**「アドレナリン」**autonomy**「自律性」**Tilburg University**「ティルブルフ大学」オランダ北ブラバント州の都市ティルブルフにある公立研究大学。1927 年創設。

❯ Questions for Understanding

Part 1 *Look at the following statements. Write T if the statement is True, and F if it is False. Write the number of the paragraph where you find the answer in the parenthesis.*

1) _____ The hormone oxytocin increases our ability to identify threats.   (   )

2) _____ If people are always happy, they are more likely to make bad decisions.

                   (   )

3) _____ It is believed that controlled aggression can help build autonomy, identity, and engagement with peers.   (   )

4) _____ Avoiding negative feelings can lead to serious consequences.   (   )

Part 2 *Look at the questions below. Check the best answer for each.*

1) What does the US army do for its soldiers?
    a. ☐ Hires happiness experts
    b. ☐ Organizes self-help courses
    c. ☐ Posts inspirational happiness quotes
    d. ☐ Provides training in positive psychology

2) According to the passage, what can anger and grumpiness help us become?
- a. ☐ More easily persuaded
- b. ☐ Better at problem solving
- c. ☐ Less understanding
- d. ☐ All of the above

3) In which of the following contexts is competition important?
- a. ☐ politics
- b. ☐ business
- c. ☐ sport
- d. ☐ All of the above

4) Which word has the closest meaning to the word "enables" in Paragraph 6 (line 57)?
- a. ☐ makes
- b. ☐ allows
- c. ☐ prohibits
- d. ☐ forces

❯ Summary

① 85 CD

Fill each space with the best word from the list below.

| issues | possible | multitude | traditionally | natural | allow |

Humans are emotional creatures. In one day, we can experience a **1)** _____ of different feelings, ranging from joy and happiness to sadness and regret. It is **2)** _____ for people to try and make their experiences and feelings as positive as **3)** _____ , but the benefits of having negative emotions should not be discounted. Repressing emotions that have **4)** _____ been viewed as negative can result in greater problems and **5)** _____ in the future. It is therefore important for people to embrace their full range of emotions and **6)** _____ themselves to feel sad every once in a while.

 **Over to You**

Choose ONE of the statements below. Prepare a short response giving your opinion.

- **A life with only good experiences would be boring.**
- **It is better for teachers to be knowledgeable than kind.**

....

....

....

....

A Full Working Week

How Long Should We Work?

❯ Useful Words

Choose a word or phrase from the list below to complete each sentence.

1. Almost all universities in Japan _____ students to take entrance exams.

2. When she joined her new company, all of her _____ made her feel very welcome.

3. Some colors are _____ emotions, for example red and anger.

4. If we are too busy, we can _____ our health.

5. In many rural areas of Japan, populations have _____ decreased.

neglect	colleagues	require	associated with	drastically

❯ Reading

② 01~08 **CD**

01 **CD**

1 How many times have you heard people say that they are working too much? The answer is probably a lot. Japan has some of the longest working hours in the world. Nearly one quarter of Japanese companies require employees to work more than 80 hours of overtime a month. Those extra hours are often

5 unpaid. Furthermore, the majority of Japanese workers do not take all of their allowed time off, and often feel guilty when they do take paid leave. Working such long hours has important consequences for both workers and companies. In view of this, the question about how long we should work needs to be asked.

02 **CD**

2 In developing countries, people work long hours as low wages mean they

¹⁰ need to work a lot to earn enough money to survive. However, that is not the case for many people in North America, Europe, and East Asia. Despite that, one in five full-time employees works more than 60 hours a week, and nearly half of the workers in the US regularly work at least 50 hours. This is despite the International Labour Organization setting a limit of 48 hours per week and a

¹⁵ maximum of eight hours a day. While people may think that working long hours displays commitment, leads to higher salaries, and increases output, it could actually be negatively impacting workers, their colleagues, and their employers.

03 CD

3 First of all, working long hours can negatively affect our health or even

²⁰ lead to death. In Japan, the term *karoshi*, which means death by overwork, is legally recognized as a cause of death. Most research agrees that regularly working long

²⁵ hours can lead to both short- and long-term health effects. Short-term

Working long hours can lead to more stress.

consequences include increased levels of fatigue, stress, and sleeping disorders. Also, people tend to pick up unhealthy lifestyle habits such as smoking, alcohol abuse, irregular diet, and lack of exercise. Long-term effects include increased risk

³⁰ of developing cardiovascular disease, reproductive disorders, and mental illnesses. Furthermore, middle-aged workers who work over 55 hours a week have poorer short-term memory and reduced ability to recall words than those who work fewer than 41 hours. This suggests that spending a lot of time at work could cause long-term brain damage or dementia.

04 CD

³⁵ **4** In addition to these health implications, long working hours often increase workplace safety risks. When workers become more tired, they are less able to concentrate. This makes them more likely to make mistakes and have accidents, which can lead to injuries. That can be costly for companies which may need to pay compensation or hire replacements while workers recover.

05 CD

⁴⁰ **5** Long working hours are also associated with problems related to work–life balance. This is especially true if the long hours are compulsory. When working a lot, people engage less in their community, neglect their social life,

and have less free time to spend with their family. This can result in lower birth rates,
45 reduced mental well-being, and lower job and life satisfaction. From 2000-2008, the French government limited the maximum number of hours people could work every week to 35, and more than half of the workforce reported being
50 happier and more able to achieve a better balance between work and family or social life.

06 CD

Working less can help improve our work-life balance.

6 Surprisingly, working long hours often does not increase productivity. Despite the long working hours common in Japan, workers there
55 have the lowest productivity among G7 nations. Productivity at work decreases sharply after working 50 hours per week, and even more drastically again after 55 hours. Additionally, not taking at least one full day off per week lowers output. Reducing work hours can especially increase productivity in creative jobs.
60 Recognized geniuses in a wide range of fields, including scientist Charles Darwin, mathematician Henri Poincaré, and inventor Thomas Jefferson, all worked for approximately four hours each day on creative tasks. Another reason working long hours can decrease productivity is that some tasks can only be done according to other people's schedules. For example, salespeople often need to
65 adjust their timetables to suit their customers.

07 CD

7 In response to increased awareness of the negatives outlined above, both Japan's government and its companies claim they are actively trying to reduce working hours. The government has implemented several initiatives, including making it mandatory to take at least five vacation days per year, increasing the
70 number of public holidays to 16, and introducing a scheme called Premium Fridays. Under this initiative, companies are encouraged to allow their employees to leave at 3 p.m. on the last Friday of every month. However, on the first Premium Friday in February 2017, fewer than 4 percent of employees in Japan actually left early.

08 CD

75 **8** The research is clear: working too many hours has an adverse effect on

workplace safety and productivity. More importantly, overwork damages both our physical and mental health, and negatively impacts our social lives. However, convincing companies and their employees to reduce their working hours is not easy, especially in cultures where working overtime is seen as normal. We must
80 work together to create a working environment that recognizes the fact that time away from work makes us all better workers.

Notes
....

take time off「休む」**The International Labour Organization**「国際労働機関」国連の専門機関。1919 年創設。**fatigue**「疲労」**sleeping disorders**「睡眠障害」**cardiovascular**「心臓血管の」**dementia**「認知症」**compensation**「補償金」**compulsory**「義務的な、必須の」**G7**（= **Group of Seven**）先進 7 か国（米・日・独・仏・英・伊・加）。**Charles Darwin**「チャールズ・ダーウィン（1809-82）」英国の博物学者。進化論を提唱した。**Henri Poincaré**「アンリ・ポワンカレ（1854-1912）」仏の数学者・物理学者。天体力学も含め重要な理論の基礎を築いた。**Thomas Jefferson**「トマス・ジェファソン（1743-1826）」米国の政治家・思想家。第 3 代大統領（1801-09）。アメリカ独立宣言の起草者であり、暗号機などの発明もしている。**implement**「施行する、実施する」**initiative**「新政策」

❯ Questions for Understanding

Part 1 *Look at the following statements about the passage. Write T if the statement is True, and F if it is False. Write the number of the paragraph where you find the answer in the parenthesis.*

1) _____ Over half of US workers work more than 50 hours a week.   (   )

2) _____ In France, more than half of the workers reported being happier when working a maximum of 35 hours a week.   (   )

3) _____ Taking at least one full day off a week increases productivity.   (   )

4) _____ It is easy to make companies and workers work fewer hours.   (   )

Part 2 *Look at the following questions about the passage. Check the best answer for each.*

1) What figure did the International Labour Organization set as a limit for working hours per week?
   a. ☐ 60
   b. ☐ 50
   c. ☐ 48
   d. ☐ 8

70

2) What can be a result of workers spending less time with their family?
   a. ☐ lower birth rates
   b. ☐ reduced mental well-being
   c. ☐ lower job and life satisfaction
   d. ☐ All of the above

3) What do salespeople often have to adjust?
   a. ☐ their productivity
   b. ☐ their timetables
   c. ☐ their customers
   d. ☐ All of the above

4) Which word has the closest meaning to the word "mandatory" in Paragraph 7 (line 69)?
   a. ☐ possible
   b. ☐ allowed
   c. ☐ compulsory
   d. ☐ encouraged

❯ Summary

② 09 CD

Fill each space with the best word from the list below.

disrupted	deteriorate	pressure	complete	whether	tempting

There are many reasons why people work long hours. Some feel
1) _____ from managers or supervisors, some have too many tasks to be
able to 2) _____ in just eight hours a day, and others enjoy their jobs and
like spending time at work. However, while spending extra time at work can be
3) _____ , people need to consider the effects that could have on their lives.
Productivity could drop, work-life balance can be 4) _____ , and health can
5) _____ . In view of this, both workers and companies should ask
themselves 6) _____ working so much is really worth it.

 **Over to You**

Choose ONE of the statements below. Prepare a short response giving your opinion.

- People should work for one company for their whole careers.
- Being happy at work is more important than earning a lot of money.

....

....

....

....

Chapter 12

Waste Not, Want Not

From Recycling to a Circular Economy

❯ Useful Words

Choose a word or phrase from the list below to complete each sentence.

1. The chef is very _____. You must try the miso and mascarpone cheese dip!

2. We were very happy when the old car park was _____ a children's park.

3. Regular practice is _____ to becoming good at any skill or sport.

4. Daily exercise can _____ improve your health.

5. I want to grow roses in my garden but the _____ is not good enough. I need to buy some fertilizer.

significantly	inventive	converted into	fundamental	soil

❯ Reading

② 10~17 CD

10 CD

1 How much rubbish do you throw away a day? How much in a week? How about in a year? Japanese people produce more than 40 million tons of garbage every year. That is nearly one kilogram per person every day. In the US, the figure is even higher, with the average American producing about two
5 kilograms of trash every day. You probably have not thought about it, but do you know what happens to your trash after you throw it away? Many people are surprised to learn that only about 20 percent of rubbish in Japan and the US is recycled. Most of the rest is burned and buried. While some countries, such as Germany and South Korea, have recycling rates of more than 50 percent, it is

10 clear that the world is still a long way from achieving a truly circular economy.

11
If you don't want to see this...

2 What is a circular economy? Put simply, it means an economy where no net waste is produced. In other words, it is a system in which all
15 rubbish is reused or recycled. But how is that possible? Let's look at a different way of thinking about garbage.

12 **3** In a circular economy, all of
20 the reusable resources are removed from garbage and used again to produce new products. As well as glass, paper, aluminum, steel, and plastic, this also includes less well-known but valuable resources, such as gold and rare earth elements from computers and phones, and platinum and palladium from the catalytic converters in cars. Doing this means
25 that businesses need much less energy to make new products. In addition, it helps to protect the environment. However, recovering these useful resources can use a lot of energy, which can significantly increase the costs of products made from recycled materials.

13 **4** One way to reduce the energy required in recycling is to burn rubbish in
30 order to produce electricity and heat. Furthermore, burning rubbish reduces its mass by up to 90 percent, which means that less space is required when disposing of the ash. However, simply burning trash is not a good solution. One reason is that if the rubbish is not burned at a high enough temperature, it will produce lots of smoke and other hazardous chemicals such as dioxins. Another
35 problem is that burning garbage produces greenhouse gases like carbon dioxide. An alternative approach is to compost food and plant waste, and to only burn trash that cannot be recycled or reused in any other way. Composting basically allows microorganisms and insects to eat the rubbish. During the composting process, methane gas is released, which can be burned as a fuel or converted into
40 various chemicals and plastics. Furthermore, some of the insects can be used as food for animals or even humans, and the final result of the composting process is a useful fertilizer for fields and gardens.

14 CD

5 Whenever garbage is burned, some carbon dioxide will be produced. One possible solution to this is carbon capture and storage, in which the carbon dioxide is stored deep underground or converted into limestone rock. Scientists are also working hard to develop ways to make use of the carbon dioxide. One possibility is to use the waste carbon dioxide gas as an ingredient in making new plastics. Another possibility is to feed the gas to algae and bacteria in order to produce useful chemicals and food.

15 CD

6 The ash that remains from burning is often buried in the ground, but it can also be reused. Ash that comes from the burning of wood or food waste can be used to improve the quality of soil. Other kinds of ash can be converted into cement, which is then turned into the concrete used by the construction industry. Ash has even been used to reclaim land from the sea. For example, much of the reclaimed land in Tokyo Bay was made from ash created by burning trash.

16 CD

7 Scientists and engineers are finding ever more inventive ways to reuse and recycle our garbage, from turning old clothes into building materials, through recycling concrete, to creating genetically modified bacteria that can eat plastic. However, there is a fundamental barrier to achieving a circular economy: us. To maximize efficiency and minimize the costs of reusing and recycling trash, we must sort it before we throw it away. Unfortunately, many people do not do this properly, and some are unwilling to do it at all. For example, in Finland, a country which is aiming to achieve a circular economy by 2025,

... then treat your garbage properly.

up to 40 percent of food waste is not correctly sorted. As a result, this waste must be burned instead of being used in a more productive way.

17 CD

8 Sorting rubbish can sometimes be a chore, and trash is not something we want to worry about once we have thrown it away. However, in order to protect the environment and reduce the effects of climate change, it is important for us to understand that taking more responsibility for our garbage can change the

| 75 world for the better.

Notes ....

net（adj.）「最終的な、正味の」rare earth element「希土類元素、レアアース」希少価値の高い元素。palladium
「パラジウム」catalytic converter「触媒コンバーター」自動車の排気ガス浄化装置。dioxin「ダイオキシン」
有毒な有機塩素化合物。carbon dioxide「二酸化炭素」compost（vt）「～を堆肥にする」microorganism「微
生物」limestone rock「石灰岩」algae「藻、藻類」

❯ Questions for Understanding

Part 1　*Look at the following statements about the passage. Write T if the statement is True, and F if it is False. Write the number of the paragraph where you find the answer in the parenthesis.*

1) ____ A circular economy is an economy that does not create any rubbish.

(　　)

2) ____ A key issue for both industry and environmental protection is energy use.

(　　)

3) ____ We must be careful not to release polluting chemicals when recycling trash.

(　　)

4) ____ It is difficult to recycle old clothes and building materials.　(　　)

Part 2　*Look at the following questions about the passage. Check the best answer for each.*

1) Which word has the closest meaning to the word "figure" in Paragraph 1 (line 4)?
a. ☐ number　b. ☐ shape　c. ☐ calculate　d. ☐ choose

2) According to the passage, why are many people surprised?
a. ☐ Because Americans produce nearly twice as much rubbish as Japanese people.
b. ☐ Because Germany and South Korea recycle less trash than Japan and the US.
c. ☐ Because about 80 percent of American and Japanese garbage is not recycled.
d. ☐ Because just four countries produce over 40 million tons of garbage every year.

3) According to the passage, what is produced as a result of composting?
    a. ☐ Fertilizer, food, and dioxins
    b. ☐ Fertilizer, fuel, and plastics
    c. ☐ Fertilizer, chemicals, and food
    d. ☐ Fertilizer, food, and methane

4) According to the passage, what is preventing us from achieving a circular economy?
    a. ☐ Recovering and recycling resources uses a lot of energy.
    b. ☐ Too few people are willing to correctly sort their trash.
    c. ☐ Recycling produces hazardous chemicals like dioxins.
    d. ☐ People worry too much about reusing and recycling rubbish.

❯ Summary

② 18 CD

Fill each space with the best word or phrase from the list below.

convert	responsibility	unwilling to	reusable	chore	fuel

Sorting rubbish is a 1) _____ that some of us are 2) _____ do, but it is essential if we want to help protect the environment. Instead of just burning or burying garbage, we can 3) _____ the 4) _____ resources it contains into a variety of useful products such as 5) _____ . By doing so, we can move closer to achieving a circular economy, which means that instead of thinking about rubbish as something that is useless, we treat it as an important and useful resource. This will help both the environment and business and ensure that we can maintain the quality of our lives without destroying the natural world. Creating a circular economy will not be easy but it is the 6) _____ of us all.

Over to You

Choose ONE of the statements below. Prepare a short response giving your opinion.

- Sorting rubbish is too much of a bother.
- We should find ways to reduce the amount of trash we throw away.

....

....

....

....

13

Try This

Why Giving Things Away Can Be Good for Business

> **Useful Words**

Choose a word from the list below to complete each sentence.

1. I've always wanted a sports car, but they are so expensive that I don't think I'll ever be able to _____ one.

2. I stayed in a hotel in Nagoya which offered all guests _____ welcome drinks.

3. Nowadays, large online shopping _____ like Black Friday and Cyber Monday are becoming more common.

4. My grandfather was a very _____ man. He donated a lot of money to charities.

5. Many people _____ money on the stock exchange in an attempt to become rich.

| promotions | generous | complimentary | afford | invest |

> **Reading**

② 19~26 CD

19 CD

1 It is often satisfying to go shopping and buy something that you really want. That feeling can be intensified if you have needed to work hard and save up to afford your purchase. What can be even better though, is if you can get an item for free. Have you ever wondered why businesses sometimes give products away? Most consumers love getting a free gift, but the companies handing out complimentary goods love their giveaways even more. When consumers receive something for free, they react in a variety of surprising ways. These reactions commonly lead to increased sales and therefore greater profits for companies.

Shopping can often make us feel good.

2 In the US, 7-Eleven hosts a Free Slurpee Day every year on July 11. People can enter a shop, order a small Slurpee, and then leave without paying any money at all. For 7-Eleven, that seems like a sure way of losing money. However, many people buy extra Slurpees that are not part of the giveaway. So, despite the company giving away 4.5 million drinks for free each year, Slurpee sales actually increase by 38 percent on average, meaning that profits rise. Why is this the case? It is called the "reciprocity principle." When customers have been given a free gift, they feel obliged to buy something. This is just one of the ways that companies can benefit from the power of giveaways.

3 In the food industry, free giveaways are common. Some restaurants offer deals where children can eat for free. Why? Because children do not eat alone. The parents that accompany them have to eat, too, and an adult's meal costs much more than a child's meal. This is also true for promotions offering free appetizers. Customers go to the restaurant for the free appetizer, but pay more for a main meal, dessert, and drinks. Another popular promotion for restaurants is to offer something for free when a customer downloads their phone application. Companies in many sectors do this because it gives them a way to contact their customers directly and encourage them to return with more special deals in the future. It also enables companies to build up databases with information about their customers and what their buying preferences are.

4 Encouraging consumers to report positively on a company or product can be just as effective in promoting sales as traditional advertising. This is especially true on social media platforms, such as Instagram. It has been claimed that people talk about products they received for free 20 percent more than those they paid for. So, maybe the best way to promote a product is to simply give it away. This is called "seeding the market." In Japan, some companies give products to teenagers for free, and in return, they promote the product at schools and clubs. This is known as word-of-mouth advertising, or *kuchikomi* in Japanese.

23 CD

5 Companies can also come to be viewed as more fun with a giveaway. If there is mystery surrounding a free gift, not only do people buy more, but they also enjoy doing so. This is particularly true when buying what researchers call "affective goods." These are goods that make you happy or feel good about yourself when buying them, such as cosmetics and perfume. Giving away an item for free can also improve the public image of that item, not just the company that produced it. If a complimentary item is added to a sale of expensive or luxury goods, consumers view that product to also be of high quality. They will then pay more for the item on its own in the future.

24 CD

6 Another factor to consider is that companies often do not give away as much as consumers think they do. In general, people are not good at calculating percentages. Experiments found that when given a choice of getting 33 percent more coffee or 33 percent off the regular price of coffee, more people picked the former, even though the discount was a better deal.

Do we really understand the discounts we are being offered?

Many companies also offer customers the chance to win a free prize, but the possibility of winning is very low. Using this to their advantage means companies can appear more generous than they really are.

25 CD

7 Offering free products can not only increase profits, it can also save companies money. Many businesses invest heavily in market research to gain insights into customers' opinions. By giving out free samples, companies can receive both instant feedback and online feedback if a hashtag or Twitter handle are visible. This is especially important for a new business or a company trying a new system.

26 CD

8 It is often stated that it is harder to gain a new customer than keep a current one, and that buyers are creatures of habit. However, people are more likely to try something new if it is free. They also behave more emotionally when

they receive a free gift. Added to the benefits in terms of image and increased
75 feedback, it is easy to see how a company gains a lot more than it loses by giving
things away.

Notes

give away「無料で渡す」**Slurpee**「スラーピー」セブンイレブンのフローズン飲料。**reciprocity principle**「相互主義」**feel obliged to**「〜しなければならないと思う」**appetizer**「前菜」**social media platform**「ソーシャルメディアプラットホーム」ソーシャルサービスやアプリケーションを提供する基盤となる SNS のこと。代表例は Facebook, Twitter など。**Instagram** Chapter 2 参照。**hashtag**「ハッシュタグ」SNS に投稿する際、＃（ハッシュマーク）をフレーズの前につけることで投稿が分類しやすくなる。**handle**「ハンドル（ネーム）」本名ではなくネット上で使用する名前。

❯ Questions for Understanding

Part 1 *Look at the following statements about the passage. Write T if the statement is True, and F if it is False. Write the number of the paragraph where you find the answer in the parenthesis.*

1) _____ On Free Slurpee Day at 7-Eleven in the US, customers can only get a free drink if they buy something else. ( )

2) _____ Adults' meals are more expensive than children's meals. ( )

3) _____ People talk about products they receive for free more than those they buy. ( )

4) _____ According to the passage most people are good at calculating percentages. ( )

Part 2 *Look at the following questions about the passage. Check the best answer for each.*

1) What do some companies collect in databases?
   a. ☐ Promotions
   b. ☐ Phone applications
   c. ☐ Special deals
   d. ☐ Information about customers

2) When "seeding the market," who do Japanese companies give products to for free?
   a. ☐ other companies
   b. ☐ teenagers
   c. ☐ schools
   d. ☐ clubs

3) Which word has the closest meaning to the word "particularly" in Paragraph 5 (line 45)?
   a. ☐ especially
   b. ☐ uniquely
   c. ☐ surprisingly
   d. ☐ unusually

4) Which of the following is <u>not</u> true of offering free products?
   a. ☐ It can increase profits.
   b. ☐ It can save companies money.
   c. ☐ Many companies invest heavily in it.
   d. ☐ It can help companies receive feedback.

❯ Summary

② 27

Fill each space with the best word from the list below.

response	charged	majority	gather	include	unexpected

The large 1) _____ of people enjoy receiving things for free, especially when they come from a(n) 2) _____ source. However, it is important to look past that initial positive 3) _____ and analyze why we have been given something without being 4) _____ for it. Free products are often more beneficial for the companies that give them than for the consumers that receive them. These benefits 5) _____ increased sales, improved public image, and the chance to 6) _____ important data about both current and possible customers.

Over to You

Choose ONE of the statements below. Prepare a short response giving your opinion.

- Advertising should not be aimed at children.
- Companies now have access to too much of our personal data.

Chapter 14

Selling Sports

The Commercialization of Sports

❯ Useful Words

Choose a word or phrase from the list below to complete each sentence.

1. _____ to Japan, the English summer is usually cooler and less humid.

2. After studying so hard for so long, she was _____ to see her results.

3. The comedian entered the talent contest in order to increase his _____ to the public.

4. The argument about which idol singer was the best became more and more _____.

5. She smoked for more than 20 years, to the _____ of her health.

---

in comparison   detriment   exposure   keen   fierce

❯ Reading

② 28~35

28 🎵

1 In the summer of 2019, the Italian soccer team Juventus played against the K League All Stars in front of 60,000 fans in Seoul, Korea. Many of those fans were keen to see the world-famous player, Cristiano Ronaldo. However, even though the contract between Juventus and Korea's K League required Ronaldo to
5 play for at least 45 minutes, in fact he did not play at all. As a result, angry Korean fans took legal action against Juventus, demanding compensation… and won.

29 🎵

2 For thousands of years, sports have been an important cultural activity. Every day, millions of people enjoy taking part in or watching sports around the world. Given this popularity, it should be no surprise that sports also have a long connection with money and power. As far back as the second century BCE, Roman politicians paid for gladiatorial contests to boost their popularity before an election. In modern times, that link has become even stronger, and sports are now a business that generates tens of billions of dollars annually. This commercialization is changing the face of sports in numerous ways.

What's *your* favorite sport?

30 🎧

3 Producing a sporting event or creating a winning team can be incredibly expensive. Consequently, as well as selling tickets and merchandise to fans, teams and sports organizations such as the International Olympic Committee also sell TV channels the right to broadcast events and sell companies advertising rights. For a company, being associated with a popular sports team or event can help to improve its brand image, and increase both exposure and sales. For example, in 1939, the Gillette company paid $100,000 to be the exclusive sponsor of the baseball World Series, and its sales increased by 350 percent. The success that sports sponsorship can bring means that there is fierce competition to become sponsors. As a result, the amount spent on sponsorship globally has increased hugely. Since the mid-1980s, it rose from $5.6 billion per year to $65.8 billion in 2018.

31 🎧

4 Many people feel that the amount of advertising in sports has gone too far. Some sports have even changed their rules so that extra commercials can be shown or so that matches fit into broadcasting schedules. For example, the NFL shortened the length of the half-time break so that games could fit into a 2.5-hour TV slot, but then increased the number of timeouts so that more commercials could be shown. While this may be good for sponsors, sometimes it can be to the detriment of the athletes competing and the paying audience.

32 🎧

5 In all professional sports, teams benefit financially from the willingness of fans to pay to watch the games and purchase the products advertised by sports

personalities. However, the true value of sports as a business is seen most
45 clearly in those professional sports with a worldwide audience, such as American football, baseball, soccer, and basketball. The Dallas Cowboys American football team is the world's
50 richest sports team with a revenue of $864 million in 2018, but they are not the only super-rich sports team. In

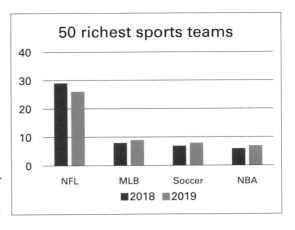

50 richest sports teams

2019, 52 teams across all sports were worth at least $2 billion, compared to just one in 2012, Manchester United Football Club.

33 CD

55 **6** A lot of money is also invested in sponsoring athletes. Hundreds of professional athletes earn more than $1 million a year, and sponsorship can make up over 90 percent of their income. While eight out of the top 15 athletes earning the most from sponsorship play individual sports, like tennis and golf, in team sports, sponsorship money is not always shared fairly. In 2019, the
60 United States Women's National Soccer Team began legal action against the United States Soccer Federation. The problem was that while the women's team attracted about the same amount of sponsorship as the men's team, the women were paid about 10 percent less. This is despite the women's team winning the FIFA Women's World Cup four times since the competition began in 1991. In
65 comparison, the best performance achieved by the men's team in the FIFA World Cup was third place in 1930.

34 CD

7 Although the financial benefits of commercialization are obvious, there are negatives. It puts athletes under increased pressure from sponsors and teams to perform well in order to generate more money. Furthermore, as fans pay more
70 and more money to watch their favorite sports, they expect the performances of the athletes to become ever more extraordinary. As a result, athletes are being forced to stretch their bodies to extremes and risk injury. In addition, they can become tempted to take drugs and cheat. This can have a profound impact on fans. While some may lose their enthusiasm for sports that are corrupt, others
75 start to believe that cheating is natural and acceptable.

8 Is the increasing commercialization of sports a problem or an opportunity? To some, commercialization brings sports to millions, and enables many people to fulfil their dreams. To others, however, sports have become more a race for money than athletes competing for the love of their sport. Ultimately, 80 it is sports fans who pay for sports, and only they can decide just how far commercialization of sports will go.

Notes

Juventus「ユヴェントス」イタリアプロサッカーリーグに加盟するフットボールクラブ。 **As far back as**「〜まで遡ると、はるか〜の昔に」**BCE = Before the Common Era**「紀元前」BC（Before Christ）と同意語だか宗教色がない表現。**gladiatorial contests**「剣闘士の試合」古代ローマでスポーツとして人気を博した。**The Gillette company**「ジレット社」世界で初めてT字型剃刀の製造販売をしたアメリカ企業。2005 年にP&Gグループに吸収合併された。**NFL = National Football League**「全米フットボール連盟」**TV slot**「テレビ番組の時間枠」**sport personalities**「有名スポーツ選手」**Dallas Cowboys**「ダラスカウボーイズ」テキサス州ダラスを本拠地とする NFL のフットボールチーム。**Manchester United**「マンチェスターユナイテッド」イングランドの名門サッカークラブ。1878 年創設。**make up**「（割合を）占める」**the United States Soccer Federation**「アメリカ合衆国サッカー連盟」**FIFA = Fédération Internationale de Football Association**（フランス語の省略）「国際サッカー連盟」**stretch their bodies to extremes**「極端なまでに身体を酷使する」

Questions for Understanding

Part 1 *Look at the following statements. Write T if the statement is True, and F if it is False. Write the number of the paragraph where you find the answer in the parenthesis.*

1) ____ Sporting events have been used to change public opinion since the second century BCE. ( )

2) ____ The NFL shortened the length of the half-time break so TV companies could show more commercials. ( )

3) ____ More than half of the top 15 athletes earning the most from sponsorship play individual sports. ( )

4) ____ Commercialization can negatively affect athletes. ( )

Part 2 *Look at the questions below. Check the best answer for each.*

1) What did 60,000 fans in South Korea do in the summer of 2019?
   a. ☐ They watched Cristiano Ronaldo play football against K League All Stars.
   b. ☐ They watched Juventus play soccer against K League All Stars.
   c. ☐ They signed a contract with Juventus.
   d. ☐ They demanded compensation from Juventus.

2) Choose the word that has the closest meaning to the word "boost" in Paragraph 2 (line 14).

a. ☐ motivate   b. ☐ increase   c. ☐ damage   d. ☐ encourage

3) Which of the following is not mentioned as a benefit of sports sponsorship for companies?

a. ☐ Creating a winning team
b. ☐ Improved image
c. ☐ Increased sales
d. ☐ Increased exposure

4) What can some fans start to do as a result of athletes becoming tempted to take drugs and cheat?

a. ☐ Pay more money to watch their favorite sport
b. ☐ Stretch their bodies to extremes
c. ☐ Risk injury
d. ☐ Believe that cheating is natural and acceptable

❯ Summary

② 36 CD

Fill each space with the best word from the list below.

compensation	ultimately	profound
commercialization	merchandise	benefit

There has been a relationship between sports and money for a long time. Recently, however, people have become concerned about the level of 1) _____ that is seen in some sports. Successful teams and athletes can earn huge amounts of money through the sale of 2) _____ and TV broadcast rights. Unfortunately, not all athletes 3) _____ equally from this revenue. Female athletes often receive less 4) _____ than male athletes, for example. This increased focus on making money is causing a 5) _____ change in the relationship between fans and the teams they love. 6) _____, fans must decide if they can continue to support sports that see them simply as customers.

Over to You

Choose ONE of the statements below. Prepare a short response giving your opinion.

- Nowadays, athletes earn too much money.
- There should be less advertising at sports events.

....

....

....

....

Paying for Information

Chapter 15

The Cost of News

❯ Useful Words

Choose a word from the list below to complete each sentence.

1. Scientists have _____ that there are four million plant and animal species in Brazil.

2. Some companies use the _____ of giving away products for free to attract customers.

3. The government will _____ a new plan that aims to reduce unemployment.

4. The population of China is _____ higher than that of the UK.

5. Despite knowing the health risks, some people _____ in smoking.

persist	strategy	implement	estimated	significantly

❯ Reading

② 37~44

37

1 How often do you check news updates online? Compare that to how often you read a newspaper. The ease with which people can connect to the
5 internet and search for stories now means that reading news online is becoming increasingly popular. This is reflected in falling sales of newspapers. In the US, daily newspaper sales are

Global sales of newspapers are decreasing rapidly.

¹⁰ estimated to have dropped from 62 million weekday subscriptions in 1990 to 31 million in 2017. Even in Japan, where newspaper circulation is one of the highest in the world, print revenues are rapidly declining. Consequently, more news providers are starting to focus on their online services.

38 CD

2 News providers have four main sources of revenue: print subscription,
¹⁵ print advertising, digital subscription, and digital advertising. Traditionally, most news providers have not charged for a digital subscription, believing that this strategy increases the income made from digital advertising. However, in a bid to counter the losses caused by decreases in newspaper sales and advertising revenues, many have begun charging for news online. They do this by erecting
²⁰ paywalls.

39 CD

3 Paywalls are systems that stop users from reading webpages for free. They have been built in three main forms. Hard paywalls make content exclusive to subscribers. By preventing non-subscribers from reading articles, the number of visitors to a website often decreases, but if a news provider has a regular number
²⁵ of loyal readers, they still make a profit. Metered (or soft) paywalls are the most common. Pioneered by *The New York Times* in 2011, this system allows users to read a set number of articles before having to pay a subscription fee. Combination paywalls differentiate between types of content. News providers place premium articles behind paywalls, while other content is offered for free.
³⁰ Developing this idea further, *The Boston Globe* now has separate websites for these two content types.

40 CD

4 Deciding whether or not to implement a paywall is a huge decision, and if publishers make the wrong choice, they risk losing readers, reducing the number of people that view their content and lowering revenues. According to
³⁵ one study, the effects of paywalls varied significantly from company to company, ranging from a 24 percent increase in total sales to a 12 percent decrease. Some paywalls have been successful. For example, *The Wall Street Journal* gained more than one million paying online users after it implemented a paywall in 2018. However, for most firms, the effect of setting up a paywall on digital sales is
⁴⁰ negative. The risk is that charges may alienate readers who have become used to free content, and that would deter advertisers. Thus, the implementation of a paywall is a strategy which may help increase revenue in the short term, but not

one that will foster future growth for news corporations or the news industry in general in the long term.

41 🎧

5 Online reader revenue is relatively reliable for individual news providers, but two main questions persist: are people willing to pay to get past more than one paywall, and do paywalls work for all kinds of providers? The evidence indicates that the answer to both questions is no. In the US, over 20 percent of newspapers now require a paying subscription for full access, but only 16 percent of Americans say they are willing to pay for any online news. Far fewer are willing to pay for a second or third subscription, especially if it costs as much as their favorite site. Also, while proving successful for major news organizations, most local news providers have struggled to attract online users. For example, only two non-national papers in the US, *The Los Angeles Times* and *The Boston Globe*, have more than 100,000 paying digital subscribers.

42 🎧

6 Despite becoming more common, charging for information online is a controversial issue. While most discussions on paywalls focus on their success or failure economically, their ethical implications must not be overlooked. In the past, the internet has been open for the general public

Should all online news be free?

to discuss relevant news issues, but paywalls are restricting the opportunity to both read and share online news. This has angered many users who claim that access to news is a fundamental right and that the public interest should be put before profit. A situation where quality news is only available to those that can afford it would have clear negative consequences in the future.

43 🎧

7 As public limited companies or publicly traded companies, news providers need to make money for their stockholders, but they also have a social responsibility to allow for equal access to news and help inform the communities they serve. Some newspapers have shown a willingness to remove their paywalls when covering urgent national news or local emergencies. *The Japan Times* did this during the Covid-19 pandemic, for example.

8 High-quality journalism is essential to the functioning of a healthy society. It ensures that readers can be informed, educated, and entertained on the subjects that affect and interest them. However, when is it the right decision to charge for information online? The implementation of paywalls helps fund reporters and journalism, but it also leads to questions regarding ethics, the right to access information, and the role and function of the press in society. While it is clear that paywalls are now an established part of online journalism and they are here to stay, news providers need to find a system that balances reader experiences and making profits.

Notes

story「記事・ニュース」 circulation「発行部数」 in a bid to ~「~しようと試みて、~するために」 paywall「ペイウォール」対価を支払ったユーザーだけが有料のウェブサイトにアクセスできる方式。 metered paywall「メーター制課金」一定量の情報は無料で、それ以上は有料になる方式。 soft pay wall は購読を決める前に、内容を確認するため限られた記事を無料で読めるシステム。 *The New York Times*『ニューヨークタイムズ』米国の大手日刊紙。1851 年創刊。 *The Boston Globe*『ボストングローブ』米 New England 地方の有力日刊紙。1872 年創刊。 *The Wall Street Journal*『ウォールストリートジャーナル』米国の経済専門日刊紙。1889 年創刊。 deter「躊躇させる」 get past「通用する、使えるようになる」 *The Los Angeles Times*『ロサンジェルスタイムズ』アメリカ西部最大の日刊紙。1881 年創刊。 the Covid-19 pandemic「新型コロナウイルス感染症パンデミック」 Covid-19 は coronavirus disease 2019 の略。2019 年 12 月、中国湖北省武漢市で新型の肺炎患者が多数報告され、世界に感染が拡大し、世界保健機関は 2020 年 3 月 11 日にパンデミック（世界的大流行）に相当すると発表した。 be here to stay「定着している」

Questions for Understanding

Part 1 *Look at the following statements. Write T if the statement is True, and F if it is False. Write the number of the paragraph where you find the answer in the parenthesis.*

1) ____ Japan has one of the highest global newspaper circulations. (   )

2) ____ Paywalls allow users to read newspapers for free. (   )

3) ____ For most firms, setting up paywalls increases digital sales. (   )

4) ____ Many internet users claim that access to news is a fundamental right. (   )

94

Part 2 *Look at the questions below. Check the best answer for each.*

1) By not charging a digital subscription, from which source did most news providers traditionally believe income would increase?
   a. ☐ Print subscriptions
   b. ☐ Print advertising
   c. ☐ Paywalls
   d. ☐ Digital advertising

2) Which word has the closest meaning to the word "premium" in Paragraph 3 (line 29)?
   a. ☐ luxury
   b. ☐ high-quality
   c. ☐ expensive
   d. ☐ unusual

3) Which type of paywall was pioneered by *The New York Times* in 2011?
   a. ☐ A hard paywall
   b. ☐ A metered paywall
   c. ☐ A combination paywall
   d. ☐ All of the above

4) Which of the following is <u>not</u> listed as a topic the implementation of paywalls can lead to questions about?
   a. ☐ Readers being entertained
   b. ☐ Ethics
   c. ☐ The right of access to information
   d. ☐ The role and function of the press in society

❯ Summary

② 45 CD

Fill each space with the best word from the list below.

potential	situations	content	reliable	domestic	deceived

Keeping up to date with international and **1)** _____ news stories is important for people to understand the societies in which they live. If access to news stories is restricted, then misinformation about many **2)** _____ can be spread a lot more easily. This can have dangerous results, such as the public being **3)** _____ or misled. However, news providers often need to make money to be able to continue investigating 4) _____ news stories and that can mean charging money for online 5) _____ . In order for users to have access to quality and 6) _____ information, sometimes paying a subscription is the best option.

❯ Over to You

Choose ONE of the statements below. Prepare a short response giving your opinion.

- **Students should discuss current news topics in their classes at school.**
- **All news on the internet should be available for free.**

....

....

....

....

Your Phone is a Soldier

What Does Cyberwar Mean?

❯ Useful Words

Choose a word or phrase from the list below to complete each sentence.

1. She wanted to develop her _____ in Chinese, so she took a class in it.

2. The typhoon damaged much of the town's _____, including both bridges and the hospital.

3. It is important to stay home if you have influenza in order to avoid _____ others.

4. Our favorite coffee shop has been _____ by noisy freshmen students!

5. After we have _____ the results from every part of the country, we will know who has won the election.

collated	infrastructure	expertise	infecting	taken over

❯ Reading

② 46~55 CD

46 CD

1 In 2009, a computer virus called Stuxnet began infecting computers used in the Iranian nuclear industry. The virus infected more than 200,000 computers and damaged or destroyed more than 1,000 machines in Iran. The era of cyberwarfare had begun.

47 CD

5 **2** Controlling information and damaging the infrastructure of the enemy are more important to winning a war than simply killing as many enemy soldiers as possible. Today, we live in a world where computers are used in nearly every industry. We navigate via GPS, and we communicate over the internet. As a

result, the information stored on computers and patterns of data on the internet can be very useful to our enemies. Consequently, it should be no surprise that warfare has come to the digital realm. What does cyberwarfare look like, who does it, and how is it used?

If you have a smartphone...

48 **CD**

3 Cyberwarfare is conducted by hacking, phishing, spoofing, or simply by analyzing publicly available data. The weapons of cyberwarfare are viruses, worms, malware, and human error. For example, in 2011 it was discovered that a group of hackers, believed to be members of the Chinese military, had successfully infiltrated

... someone may be using it to spy on you.

and stolen information from at least 70 organizations, including businesses involved in defense and the United Nations. It is believed that the hackers began their operation in 2006, and that they are still active today. Here are some more examples of cyberwarfare.

49 **CD**

4 In April 2015, a group of Russian hackers, suspected of being connected to Russian military intelligence, used malware to stop 12 channels of the TV5 French television network broadcasting for three hours. In addition, the network's intranet and email systems were closed down, and the company's social media accounts were also taken over and used to broadcast personal information about the families of French soldiers fighting against the ISIS terrorist group. The hackers were able to do all of this because TV5 had accidentally revealed some of their usernames and passwords during a television interview; they were on the wall behind the interviewee. In 2016, the same group modified an app used by the Ukranian military to control some of their D-30 howitzers, resulting in the destruction of 20 percent of the weapons.

50 **CD**

5 In June 2017, more than 20 ships sailing in the Black Sea, between Russia and Turkey, discovered that their GPS readings were incorrect. In fact, they were up to 32 kilometers off course. It is widely believed that this incident was the result of the Russian government testing a cyberweapon that spoofs GPS signals. In March 2015, Iranian hackers shut down the power grid in 44 of Turkey's 81 provinces, leaving 40 million people without power for 12 hours. In 2019, it was revealed that Russian hackers had infiltrated the US national power grid, and that US hackers had done the same to the Russians.

51

6 Social media can also be useful for cyberwarfare. During 2015 and 2016, Russian agents created social media feeds that sought to divide Americans politically and ensure the election of Donald Trump. In one case, a protest at an Islamic center in Texas in May 2016, it was discovered that the Russians had used social media to organize *both* sides of the protest. In 2017, it was estimated that 150 million Americans had seen Russian-generated advertisements on Facebook during the 2016 US presidential election.

52

7 Even publicly available data can aid cyberwarriors, as this example shows. Millions of people around the world use the popular Strava app to record their exercise routines, such as cycling and jogging routes. In November 2017, Strava released a map which collated all the data produced by its users. In January 2018, it was realized that this data included that of soldiers and that, as a result, the locations and layouts of US military bases around the world had been revealed.

53

8 One of the attractions of cyberwarfare is this: it is cheap. Often all that is needed is a computer, an internet connection, and some programming expertise. Furthermore, once an attack has been launched, the code can often be analyzed and used in different ways. For example, a modified version of the Stuxnet virus was employed to switch off the safety systems in a Saudi Arabian power station in December 2017. It is widely believed that Iranian hackers were behind the attack.

54

9 How can we protect ourselves from cyberwarfare? For individuals, companies, and government agencies, the advice is surprisingly the same: keep software up to date, use reliable antivirus software, and practice good security with passwords. However, for whole countries the only answer may be to disconnect from the global internet if a cyberattack begins. This was something

⁷⁵ that Russia tested in 2019, and countries such as Iran and China are also attempting to ensure that their internet can survive being disconnected in this way.

55 🎧CD

10 It is perhaps ironic that the internet, a computer system designed in the 20th century to allow the US military to continue functioning during a nuclear
⁸⁰ war, has become a battleground of the 21st century. It remains to be seen if the online world that has developed based on the principles of openness and freedom can survive the threat of cyberwarfare.

Notes

Stuxnet「スタックスネット」標的型の有害なソフトウェア。インターネットに接続していない状態でも USB などを経由して感染する。**cyberwarfare**「サイバー戦争」**phishing**「フィッシング」金融機関などを装い、電子メールやウェブサイトを使って暗証番号などの個人情報を不正に入手する詐欺。**spoofing**「なりすまし」他人のアドレスやサイトを偽造して騙す行為。**worm**「ワーム」コンピューターのシステムに侵入して破壊や情報漏洩を行うプログラム。**malware**「マルウェア」有害なソフトウェアの総称。**military intelligence**「軍事情報部」**TV5**（= **TV5 MONDO**）「テヴェサンクモンド」フランス国際放送。**intranet**「イントラネット」企業内コンピューターネットワーク。**ISIS**（= **Islamic State of Iraq and Syria**）イスラム過激派組織。**D-30 howitzer**「D-30 榴弾砲」火砲の一種。射程距離は短いが、遮蔽物を越えて射撃できる。**power grid**「配電網」**feed**「フィード」ウェブサイトの更新情報や記事などを配信するためにまとめたデータ。**Donald Trump**「ドナルド・トランプ（1946-)」第 45 代アメリカ大統領。**Strava**「ストラバ」米国企業 Strava Inc. が開発したアスリート向けのソーシャルネットワーク。

❯ Questions for Understanding

Part 1 *Look at the following statements about the passage. Write T if the statement is True, and F if it is False. Write the number of the paragraph where you find the answer in the parenthesis.*

1) _____ According to the passage, the original Stuxnet virus was an Iranian cyberattack. (   )

2) _____ From 2006, Russian hackers stole data from more than 70 business and government organizations. (   )

3) _____ One cyberwarfare tactic is to be both for and against a topic on social media. (   )

4) _____ If a cyberattack happens, some countries are planning to disconnect from the internet. (   )

Part 2   *Look at the following questions about the passage. Check the best answer for each.*

1) How were Russian hackers able to shut down 12 channels of TV5 in 2015?
   - a. ☐ They modified an app used by French soldiers and their families.
   - b. ☐ They used passwords that TV5 had broadcast by mistake.
   - c. ☐ They connected TV5 to Russian military intelligence.
   - d. ☐ They used the social media accounts of TV5 and ISIS.

2) Which word has the closest meaning to the word "active" in Paragraph 3 (line 28)?
   - a. ☐ functioning   b. ☐ producing   c. ☐ dynamic   d. ☐ online

3) What was unusual about the 2016 protest in Texas?
   - a. ☐ More than 150 million Americans saw advertisements for the protest.
   - b. ☐ Russian hackers organised the protest to ensure that Donald Trump was elected.
   - c. ☐ The protest was started by Russian hackers in a Texan Islamic center.
   - d. ☐ Protestors for and against the Texan Islamic center had been organised by Russians.

4) What problem was caused by the Strava app in 2017?
   - a. ☐ It was possible to make maps of American military bases by using its data.
   - b. ☐ It was discovered that Strava was an Iranian-made version of the Stuxnet virus.
   - c. ☐ Hackers spoofed the data causing cyclists and joggers to go off course.
   - d. ☐ ISIS terrorists used the data to stalk American joggers and cyclists.

▶ Summary

② 56 CD

Fill each space with the best word from the list below.

modified	conducted	realm	subtle	provinces	infiltrate

As the internet has become an essential part of our daily lives, we should not be surprised that warfare has also spread to the digital 1) _____. There are many ways that cyberwarfare can take place. Obvious cyberattacks include when Iran used cyberwarfare to shut down the power supply in more than half of Turkey's 2) _____ in 2015, and when Russian hackers 3) _____ an app in order to destroy weapons used by the Ukrainian military.

4) _____ cyberattacks include when foreign hackers 5) _____ our government computer systems and copy important data and when foreign countries use social media campaigns to disrupt our societies. Since we all use the internet, we are all targets of cyberwarfare, and so we must understand how cyberwarfare is 6) _____ and learn how to defend ourselves and our nations from cyberattacks.

❯ Over to You

Choose ONE of the statements below. Prepare a short response giving your opinion.

- **Does the idea of cyberwarfare make you worried?**
- **The government should do more to protect this country from cyberwarfare.**

....

....

....

....

The Perils of Perception

How Much Do We Really Know?

❯ Useful Words

Choose a word from the list below to complete each sentence.

1. Their dog is nice, but it can be _____ friendly sometimes.

2. Since her homemade chocolate was a _____, she decided to buy some instead.

3. He enjoyed learning English at school. _____, he decided to become an English teacher.

4. Even though we saw him take the money he continued to _____ it.

5. She hates to lose, so sometimes she _____ to make sure she wins.

cheats	deny	failure	overly	consequently

❯ Reading

② 57~63 CD

57 CD

1 How much do you know about the world? Look at the questions below and try to think of the answers.

5

What percentage of the world's people are poor? _____
What percentage of the world's people can read and write? _____
What percentage of the world's children get vaccinated? _____
What percentage of the world's land is protected? _____

Do you think it is important to know the answers to questions like these? Why?

58 CD

2 Unfortunately, we cannot be experts in every topic. As a result, we must

10 rely on other people to help inform us about the world. For most of us, that means that our biggest sources of information are our friends and the news media. However, the way that news is reported and the ways in which humans naturally think often result in our developing inaccurate opinions about the world.

59 CD

15 **3** In the 1950s, psychologists conducted many investigations into how people make decisions. In one experiment, two groups of students from different universities were shown an American football game and asked to count how often each team had broken the rules. At the end of the game, the students reported that one team had committed twice as many infractions as the other

20 team. Interestingly, both groups of students had watched the same game, and the team that they identified as cheating more was the team from the other university. In other words, the students' support for one team or the other had unconsciously affected their reports. This effect, where we interpret information so that it fits with the ideas or opinions that we already have, is known as

25 cultural cognition.

60 CD

4 One of the dangers of cultural cognition is that it can cause us to reject information that challenges the ideas and opinions that we already have. Furthermore, the more important those ideas are to our identity, the more strongly we reject information that indicates we may be wrong. A good example

30 of this is climate change. While there is no doubt among scientists that climate change is occurring, that is not a message that is accepted by certain groups in society. These groups tend to be supporters of right-wing political parties, which have tended to emphasize the importance of economic development over environmental protection. Consequently, to accept that climate change is a real

35 problem that has been caused by humanity means that ideas about politics and the relative importance of business and environmental issues also have to change. It is easier and more comfortable for such people to simply deny the idea of climate change.

61 CD

5 In 2019, eight passenger aircraft crashed. Each case was a tragedy and

40 widely reported in the media worldwide. However, are eight plane crashes a lot? After all, how many passenger plane flights were there in 2019? In fact, there were about 39 million passenger plane flights during 2019. So why do we

remember the crashes and not the safe flights? We are naturally attracted to dramatic stories because this is something that helped our species to survive in
45 the past. This is because we can often learn more from another person's failure than we can from their success. Consequently, we are interested in – and remember – bad news more than good news, and the news media tend to report more bad news as a result. In fact, when the Russian news website *The City Reporter* reported only good news for one day in 2014, the number of readers
50 dropped by two thirds.

62

6 The problem with our natural bias towards bad news lies in how news is reported. A big disaster like a plane crash is reported by every news
55 outlet, and the story is often repeated and discussed over several days. While this informs us, it also means that we enormously overestimate how common events like plane crashes are.

In some cultures, people enjoy swimming in icy water in the winter...

60 This can result in our having ideas about the world that are both incorrect and overly negative, such as the answers many people give to the questions in paragraph one. For example, in 1918, 67.1 percent of the world's population lived in extreme poverty. In 2019, that figure was 10.7 percent. Here are some other examples: global literacy reached 86 percent in 2016, the percentage of
65 children getting one or more vaccinations rose from 22 percent in 1980 to 88 percent in 2016, and the amount of the world's land that is protected increased from 0.03 percent in 1900 to 14.7 percent by 2016.

63

7 Throughout our lives we make political, economic, and social
70 decisions that have an impact on the world. However, the opinions and ideas which lead to those decisions are inevitably based on incomplete information. Understanding that there
75 are flaws in the ways we learn and think is essential if we wish to have a

... while in others a hot bath is preferred. Which one feels "right" to you?

better understanding of the world. This means that we need to seek out a more balanced view of the world than the media presents us. Then, in order to make better decisions, we must actively challenge the strongly held ideas and opinions of both ourselves and of those around us. As the philosopher Socrates is believed to have said, the first step to wisdom is accepting that, "I know nothing except the fact of my ignorance."

80

Notes

infraction「反則」cultural　cognition「文化的認知」地域等の文化背景をもとに、社会生活を営むなかで無意識のうちに身につけられるもので、価値観や行動の規範と結びつく。bias「（心の）傾向、偏見」outlet「放送局」literacy「識字能力」Socrates「ソクラテス」古代ギリシャの哲学者。弟子のプラトン等による著作を通じて彼の思想が伝えられている。

❯ Questions for Understanding

Part 1　*Look at the following statements about the passage. Write T if the statement is True, and F if it is False. Write the number of the paragraph where you find the answer in the parenthesis.*

1) ＿＿ According to the passage, we cannot obtain all the information we need by ourselves.　　　　　　　　　　　　　　　　　　　　（　　）

2) ＿＿ We tend to judge new information based on how well it fits with what we already know.　　　　　　　　　　　　　　　　　　　　（　　）

3) ＿＿ Sometimes people reject new ideas because changing their opinions is too much effort.　　　　　　　　　　　　　　　　　　　　（　　）

4) ＿＿ The popularity of *The City Reporter* website increased when it reported only good news.　　　　　　　　　　　　　　　　　　　　（　　）

Part 2　*Look at the following questions about the passage. Check the best answer for each.*

1) Which of the following best describes the 1950s American football experiment?
　a. ☐ One group of students watched two different games and had the same opinions about both of them.
　b. ☐ One group of students watched the same game twice but had different opinions about it each time.
　c. ☐ Two groups of students watched two different games and both groups had the same opinions about the games.
　d. ☐ Two groups of students watched the same game but had very different opinions about it.

2) Which word has the closest meaning to the word "interpret" in Paragraph 3 (line 23)?

a. ☐ think   b. ☐ represent   c. ☐ explain   d. ☐ analyze

3) According to the passage, why are we attracted to bad news?

a. ☐ Because bad news is often much less dramatic than good news.
b. ☐ Because we can learn more from bad news than we can from good news.
c. ☐ Because bad news is widely reported in the media worldwide.
d. ☐ Because bad news is easier to remember than good news.

4) Based on the information in the passage, which of the following is correct?

a. ☐ Around one quarter of world's land was protected in 2016.
b. ☐ Global poverty increased by roughly one tenth in 2019.
c. ☐ Almost nine tenths of children were vaccinated in 2016.
d. ☐ About two thirds of people could read and write in 2016.

▶ Summary

② 64 CD

Fill each space with the best word or phrase from the list below.

relying on	reject	species
inevitably	overestimate	inaccurate

One reason for the success of our 1) _____ is our ability to learn from not only our own mistakes but also from the mistakes of others. By 2) _____ others to share information with us, we can learn more and more quickly than if we have to learn everything by ourselves. This 3) _____ means that we are more interested in bad news than good news and that we find it difficult to ignore a dramatic story. Unfortunately, while this has been a useful and helpful feature of human thinking, in the modern world it can lead us to 4) _____ how common events like disasters are. Furthermore, because we prefer to learn from people and news sources that we trust, we often 5) _____ or deny ideas or opinions that do not match our own. Understanding how we learn and how we can go wrong can help us to avoid forming 6) _____ opinions.

▶ Over to You

Choose ONE of the statements below. Prepare a short response giving your opinion.

- It is important to listen to the ideas of people who disagree with you.
- I think more good news should be reported.

....

....

....

....

It's a Man's World

The Cost of Ignoring Women's Needs

❯ Useful Words

Choose a word or phrase from the list below to complete each sentence.

1. After trying to have a child for five years, she finally became _____.

2. We will interview the best three _____ for the job.

3. Some people think that Android phones are _____ Apple's iPhones.

4. She was given a _____ because her ideas had been so successful.

5. In order to pass this class, your _____ in activities is necessary.

| pregnant | applicants | promotion | participation | inferior to |

❯ Reading

② 65~72 CD

65 CD

1 Try this challenge. Write the names of as many politicians as you can in one minute. Now look carefully at your list. How many of those
5 politicians are women? According to the World Bank, in 2018 the global proportion of politicians who were female averaged 24 percent. Among OECD countries in 2018, the average
10 proportion of female researchers in STEM (science, technology,

Unrepresentative: the Japanese government of 2019 included 22 men but only two women.

engineering, and mathematics) subjects was 30 percent, and 45 percent of doctors were women. In Japan, however, only 10 percent of politicians, 15 percent of STEM researchers, and 21.1 percent of doctors were female. In fact, in their 2018 report on gender equality, the World Economic Forum ranked Japan in 110th place – out of 149 countries. Despite making up half of the population, women are often under-represented in many areas of society. Why is this the case, and what is the result of the lack of representation of women in society?

66 CD

2 When humans first began farming, the ownership of land and property became important. Since children would usually inherit the property of their parents, controlling who married whom, and who had children with whom, also became important. Unfortunately, this often resulted in women being treated as a kind of property. Consequently, for nearly 12,000 years, religious and cultural traditions have tended to limit women's freedom and participation in society. It is only in the last few hundred years that the idea of women's equality has been taken seriously, with most improvements – such as women's right to vote – being achieved during the 20th century.

67 CD

3 Today, inequality for women is perpetuated in two ways: sexism and organizational blind spots. Together, sexism and organizational blind spots have huge negative effects on women's lives around the world. Sexism is the result of some people, both men and women, continuing to believe incorrect ideas that women are inferior to men. One way that sexism reduced women's power in society was by limiting their access to education. This continued until surprisingly recently. The first female students entered Tokyo University in 1946, Yale University in 1969, Harvard College in 1977, and Columbia College in 1981. In 2018, it was discovered that Tokyo Medical University had been manipulating entrance exam scores in order to reduce the number of successful female applicants.

68 CD

4 Another effect of sexism is that it encourages women to be judged on their appearance rather than their ability. For example, in 2019, Teresa Bellanova became Italy's first female Agriculture Minister. Many reporters chose to comment on the dress she wore rather than on her accomplishment. Such comments are rarely made about the appearance of male politicians or businessmen. This double standard makes it harder for women to become

45 politicians, to win promotions, or to challenge sexual harassment.

69 CD

5 Organizational blind spots mean that, because women are less common in business and academia, the necessity to include women and consider their needs are unconsciously disregarded. For example, since they are the ones that get pregnant and give birth, women inevitably spend more time involved with

50 childcare than men. However, since most politicians and business leaders are men, they rarely consider the needs of women with children, resulting in a shortage of good childcare available for working parents. For instance, in 2019, Kenyan politician Zuleika Hassan caused a scandal by taking her baby into parliament because the government building did not have a day care center. This

55 lack of childcare makes it harder for mothers to return to full-time work. As a result, most part-time workers are women, their average earnings are less than men's, and women are under-represented in governments and the upper management of companies.

70 CD

6 In March 2019, the American

60 space agency NASA had to cancel the first women-only spacewalk because the International Space Station only had medium and large-sized spacesuits while one of the female astronauts

65 needed a small-sized spacesuit. A more down-to-earth example is that car seats and seatbelts are designed for an "average" person who is 1.77m tall and weighs 76kg. In other words, an

70 average man. As a result, a woman is

During the Covid-19 pandemic, many female health workers discovered that essential personal protective equipment did not fit them well beause it was designed for men.

47 percent more likely to be seriously injured and 17 percent more likely to die in a car crash than a man.

71 CD

7 Smartphones allow us to use and enjoy the latest technology. However, they are designed to fit the average male hand, making them just a little too big

75 for most women to comfortably use one-handed. In 2014, Apple Inc. released a health-monitoring app which was able to track many different health measurements. However, it could not be used to track a woman's monthly

periods. In 2016, it was found that Google's speech-recognition software was 70 percent more likely to recognize male voices than female voices.

72 CD

80   **8** From sexists deliberately blocking women's university entry through to designers not thinking what sized spacesuits women may need, not fully representing and involving women in all areas of society results in their discomfort, disparagement, danger, and death. In the 21st century we cannot continue to treat the needs of half of our population as less important than the
85   other half. Look around the room. How many women are there? How many *should* there be? Now, what are *you* going to do about it?

Notes
....

The World Bank「世界銀行」国際復興開発銀行と国際開発協会による国際金融機関。途上国政府への融資、技術協力、政策助言を行う。1944 年設立。**OECD**（= **Organization for Economic Cooperation and Development**)「経済協力開発機構」1961 年発足。**under-represented**「不当に数が少ない、十分な代表数がない」**sexism**「（特に女性に対する）性差別」**blind   spot**「盲点、弱点」**Yale   University**「イェール大学」米 **Connecticut** 州にある私立大学。1701 年創立。**Harvard College**   Harvard University と同じであるが、大学院のない一般教養科目を履修する学部教育の機関。**Columbia College** コロンビア大学の教養学部。＊ Harvard College を参照。**double standard**「二重基準」性差などにより不公平な基準を設けること。**spacewalk**「宇宙遊泳」**down-to-earth**「実際的な、現実的な」**speech-recognition**「音声認識」**disparagement**「誹謗、軽視」

❯ Questions for Understanding

Part 1   *Look at the following statements about the passage. Write T if the statement is True, and F if it is False. Write the number of the paragraph where you find the answer in the parenthesis.*

1) _____ According to the passage, many cultures have acted to limit women's roles in society.   (   )

2) _____ Sexism means that people do not believe that women are inferior to men.   (   )

3) _____ We do not often discuss how good-looking male politicians or businessmen are.   (   )

4) _____ Many women are blocked from full-time work because there is not enough childcare.   (   )

Part 2   *Look at the following questions about the passage. Check the best answer for each.*

1) Which of the following was the last to admit female students?
   a. ☐ Tokyo University   b. ☐ Columbia College
   c. ☐ Yale University   d. ☐ Harvard College

2) According to the passage, why are women more at risk than men while driving?
   a. ☐ Because cars are designed for male bodies rather than for female bodies.
   b. ☐ Because female bodies are 47 percent smaller than male bodies.
   c. ☐ Because women have more down-to-earth bodies than men.
   d. ☐ Because male bodies are 17 percent larger than female bodies.

3) Which word has the closest meaning to the word "inevitably" in Paragraph 5 (line 49)?
   a. ☐ unnecessarily
   b. ☐ fatefully
   c. ☐ involuntarily
   d. ☐ unavoidably

4) According to the passage, what was the issue with Apple Inc.'s health-monitoring app?
   a. ☐ The app was difficult for most women to use with one hand.
   b. ☐ The app was more likely to recognise male voices than female voices.
   c. ☐ The app did not track important aspects of women's health.
   d. ☐ The app was not as good as the Google app at tracking health measurements.

❯ Summary

② 73 CD

Fill each space with the best word or phrase from the list below.

sexism	accomplishments	under-represented
property	perpetuate	blind spots

Although half of all people are women, they are 1) _____ in academia, business, and government. This is the result of cultural and religious traditions that have treated women as 2) _____ for millennia. Although things are changing, 3) _____ is still a major problem today. Just consider how often women are judged on their appearance rather than on their 4) _____, or how often women's ideas, opinions, and ambitions are met with criticism and disparagement. The lack of female representation results in political and economic

5) _____ that range from shortages in childcare through to smartphones that are too big and health apps that cannot track women's health issues. We cannot continue to 6) _____ this injustice.

❯ Over to You

Choose ONE of the statements below. Prepare a short response giving your opinion.

- **We do not need to change society because men are better than women.**
- **What advice would you give to an ambitious female relative or friend?**

....

....

....

....

Chapter 19

Changing Perceptions

Can a Country Change the Way It's Viewed?

❯ Useful Words

Choose a word or phrase from the list below to complete each sentence.

1. As we mature, the way we _____ the world can change a lot.

2. Cars made in Germany have a _____ for being reliable.

3. Between 2015 and 2018, Aoyama Gakuin University won four _____ Tokyo-Hakone ekiden races.

4. To win the competition, the chess player needed to _____ all of his opponent's weaknesses.

5. In order to be successful, companies need to _____ the hard work of their employees.

---

consecutive   reputation   perceive   exploit   rely on

❯ Reading

② 74~81

74

1 If you have an interview, it is important to dress appropriately. Wearing damaged jeans and a T-shirt would not make the right impression at an interview for a bank job, for example. Appearance has a strong impact on the way people are perceived, and a change of clothes can drastically alter a person's
5 image. For places, changing the way that they are viewed is not as simple, but it can be equally as important. It can affect all aspects of society, from business and politics to culture and tourism. Therefore, a lot of money is often invested in positively influencing the way a country is seen internationally.

2 Changing the image of a country to promote it is known as "nation branding." It is a process that is becoming more common as nations compete to attract tourists, companies, highly-skilled workers, and other talented people. According to author Peter Van Ham, enhancing a nation's image and reputation is becoming an essential part of economic development. Countries that do not engage in nation branding can have problems drawing visitors and investment.

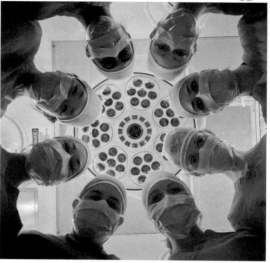

Many countries compete to attract highly-skilled workers.

3 Today, Spain has a healthy economy and is a popular tourist destination. However, until 1978, it was isolated from most of Europe, and did not have a good reputation for doing business. To change this, the country actively promoted its culture and heritage at national, regional, and global levels. Hosting sporting events, like the 1992 Barcelona Olympics, building emblematic buildings like the Guggenheim Museum in Bilbao, and encouraging Spanish multinational companies to expand all helped to improve the way the nation was viewed. The example of Spain being able to attain so much in a short time shows that nation branding can lead to success.

4 However, despite the large amounts of money that are spent on nation branding, some researchers argue whether it is actually possible for a country to change the way it is viewed. Nation branding can only do so much in promoting a country, and the case of Spain is rare, with many more examples of failed attempts than successful ones. Why is it so difficult?

Could you choose just one image to promote all of Japan?

One reason is that it is very complex. A nation has many images and associations including geography, people, history, and culture. For example, Japan could make people think of Mt. Fuji, samurai, temples, or manga. Many branding
45 campaigns aim to develop a single image that can be used to promote all of those different associations. Those campaigns often fail, as attempting to include all parts of a country in one image is almost impossible.

78 CD

5 Another point is that many of the stereotypes and cultural associations regarding a nation have long histories. Therefore, they are not easy to change. In
50 addition, some perceptions are more difficult to change than others. If a country is viewed as dangerous, it is extremely challenging to change those perceptions. One example of this is the Middle Eastern country of Jordan. Although Jordan is stable, it is located in a region that has experienced many conflicts. Consequently, it is not considered a safe vacation destination or market to invest
55 in. In an attempt to change this, the Jordanian government is working with Turkish Airlines to help assure visitors of the country's safety and the fantastic experiences they would have in Jordan. Turkish Airlines was selected because it has a strong reputation in the region and won the award for being Europe's Best Airline for six consecutive years from 2011-2016.

79 CD

60 **6** Distinctiveness is another factor that a nation brand must consider as it needs to be able to differentiate the country enough from its competitors to create an advantage. However, distinctiveness and exclusivity are hard to protect as no nation can claim to own the qualities it is seeking to promote. This has been seen with companies in the Hong Kong clothing industry using Italian
65 names, such as Giordano, to exploit Italy's reputation for fashion despite having no connection to the country.

80 CD

7 When promoting a country, a nation brand must represent the true spirit and shared values of the people of that country. This is not always achieved, however, and in some cases the portrayal of a country can even be insulting or
70 offensive to its people. In an attempt to move away from a strong connection to the past, the "Cool Britannia" campaign was launched in Britain in the 1990s. It is generally agreed it was unsuccessful. The problem was that a large part of the British population was not interested in the cutting-edge fashion, design, music, and art that was being highlighted. Also, many of the traditional characteristics

75 associated with the country and British industries, such as honor and reliability, had been excluded.

81 CD

8 Some people believe that a nation's image can be changed and promoted in a professional way which will lead to a number of benefits. Others argue that there are too many external factors that cannot be controlled. This can prevent 80 nation branding from being truly impactful and successful. Despite these different positions, both groups do agree that nation branding is now a well-established practice and that huge sums of money will continue to be spent on it.

Notes
....

talented「才能のある、有能な」 **emblematic**「象徴的な」 **The Guggenheim Museum**「グッゲンハイム美術館」ニューヨークにある同名の美術館が事業展開して創設した。1997 年開館。**Bilbao**「ビルバオ」スペイン北部の都市。**Jordan**「ヨルダン」公式名は Hashemite Kingdom of Jordan。アジア南西部の王国。1946 年独立。**Turkish Airlines**「ターキッシュ・エアラインズ」トルコの国営航空会社。**distinctiveness**「特殊性」 **exclusivity**「排他性」**Giordano**「ジョルダーノ」 **Cool Britannia**「クール・ブリタニア」1990 年代に英国文化を国内外に宣揚するめたに使われたフレーズ。国家ブランド戦略として推進された。**cutting-edge** Chapter 8 参照。 **well-established**「定着した、ゆるぎのない」

❯ Questions for Understanding

Part 1 *Look at the following statements about the passage. Write T if the statement is True, and F if it is False. Write the number of the paragraph where you find the answer in the parenthesis.*

1) _____ According to the passage, nation branding is becoming more common.

( )

2) _____ Before 1978, Spain did not have a positive business reputation. ( )

3) _____ Many stereotypes and cultural associations have long histories. ( )

4) _____ The Cool Britannia campaign included traditional characteristics associated with the UK, such as honor and reliability. ( )

Part 2 *Look at the following questions about the passage. Check the best answer for each.*

1) What helped improve the way Spain was viewed?
  a. ☐ Hosting sporting events
  b. ☐ Building emblematic buildings
  c. ☐ Encouraging Spanish multinational companies to expand
  d. ☐ All of the above

2) Why is nation branding so difficult?

    a. ☐ It is very expensive.

    b. ☐ It can change the way a country is viewed.

    c. ☐ It is very complex.

    d. ☐ Countries do not have many images or associations.

3) Complete the following sentence. According to the passage, Jordan

_____.

    a. ☐ is stable

    b. ☐ has many conflicts

    c. ☐ is unsafe

    d. ☐ has a strong reputation

4) Which word has the closest meaning to the phrase "cutting-edge" in Paragraph 7 (line 73)?

    a. ☐ dangerous

    b. ☐ modern

    c. ☐ outside

    d. ☐ external

❯ Summary

② 82 CD

Fill each space with the best word from the list below.

consequently	negative	relation
influence	experiences	previously

People usually judge how much they like something in 1) _____ to how much they expected they would like it. Therefore, 2) _____ held perceptions affect our responses to our 3) _____. They also impact on our decision making. If we have 4) _____ ideas relating to a country, we often will not travel there. 5) _____, countries spend huge amounts of money trying to positively 6) _____ the way that they are viewed. While this may sound like a simple idea, nation branding is actually very complicated.

Over to You

Choose ONE of the statements below. Prepare a short response giving your opinion.

- First impressions are very important.
- Countries should spend less money on nation branding.

It's the Law

Chapter

20

Identifying Good and Bad Laws

> **Useful Words**

Choose a word or phrase from the list below to complete each sentence.

1. Eating well and exercising regularly are _____ to good health.

2. Her brother's wedding ceremony will _____ in Hawaii.

3. He was _____ joining the gym because of his many tattoos.

4. She _____ told her father that she was studying at a friend's house when she was really on a date.

5. Not doing your homework because you were playing games all night is not a _____ excuse.

---

falsely   fundamental   barred from   take place   valid

> **Reading**

② 83~88

83 🎧

1 In April 1963, the civil rights activist Martin Luther King Jr. wrote a letter to his friends and supporters. At the time, he was in jail in the city of Birmingham, in the US state of Alabama. He had been arrested for protesting against the segregation and oppression of black people in America. In his now
5 famous *Letter from a Birmingham Jail*, King quoted a fifth century Christian writer, Augustine of Hippo, writing that, "An unjust law is no law at all." In other words, if a law is bad, we should not obey it. But how can we tell if a law is good or bad? Perhaps if we look at some examples from around the world we can discover how.

2 *Government by the People* –
The basic principle of an election is simple: the people of the country choose representatives who will make laws on their behalf. Then, every few years the people decide if they should change their representatives. Not everyone is allowed to vote, however. Children do not have the education or

What would make *you* protest?

maturity to make political decisions. Some people who are mentally ill are also barred from voting because their decision-making ability has been affected by their illness. Furthermore, until very recently many countries also had laws that only allowed men to vote. Women struggled and fought for many years to achieve universal suffrage and to be able to influence the laws that controlled them. Women first won the right to vote in 1893 in New Zealand, in 1920 in the United States, and in 1947 in Japan. But it was not until 2015 that women in Saudi Arabia became able to vote.

3 *The Consent of the Governed* –
One of the fundamental principles in society is that of consent. A democratic government only has the power that the people have voluntarily chosen to give it. A contract is an agreement between two parties, which is why it is a crime for someone to falsely use your name in a contract. In the same

Is *she* old enough to get married?

way, sexual harassment is a crime because the victims have not given their permission to be treated in a sexual manner. But what about getting married? A marriage requires consent from both parties, but when should you be allowed to get married? Globally, about 21 percent of women are married under the age of 18. These marriages mostly take place in developing nations in Africa and Asia, but they also happen elsewhere. In the United States between 2000 and 2015, more than 200,000 children got married. The youngest were only 10 years old. By 2019, only two of the 50 US states had banned child marriage. Furthermore, in those same states a person must be over 18 in order to get a divorce. Can a person who is considered too young to vote, drive, work, or even sign up to social media like Facebook, really be old enough to get married… but not old enough to get divorced?

86

4   *All Human Beings are Born Free and Equal* – Many countries have struggled to apply this basic concept. For example, until 1967 it was illegal for people of different races to get married in many US states. In Japan, the Eugenic Protection Law resulted in more than 16,000 people being sterilized between 1948 and 1996 because they had a disability. In 2019, the Japanese government officially apologized for their mistreatment.

87

5   *Freedom of Speech* – One of the ways that societies progress is through the discussion of problems and finding solutions for them. Consequently, being able to talk freely about issues is an important right. Nearly all countries limit this right in order to stop people from encouraging hatred and violence. Unfortunately, some countries go much further than this. In several countries, it is a crime to criticize the head of state. In Thailand, for example, you can be sent to prison for up to 15 years if you insult the king. Other countries try to limit the information available to their people by banning books, blocking internet sites, and imprisoning journalists. About a quarter of countries have laws that ban the criticism of religion, and some countries even tell their people what religion they can have. In 13 countries around the world, including Malaysia, Pakistan, and Saudi Arabia, not believing in any gods is a capital crime.

88

6   Having looked at some examples, we can clearly say what a bad law is. A bad law limits the rights and the power of people without a valid reason. A bad law prevents us from asking questions about ideas or our leaders. A bad law is one that causes harm. As Martin Luther King Jr. said, "Any law that uplifts human personality is just. Any law that degrades human personality is unjust." Now that we know how to identify bad laws, we must act to change them.

....

the civil rights activist「公民権運動活動家」1950-60年代アメリカで黒人が白人と同等の地位を求めて公民権運動（the civil rights movement）を展開した。その運動に積極的に賛同し行動した者。**Martin Luther King Jr.**「マーティン・ルーサー・キング・ジュニア（1929-1968）」公民権運動を指導した黒人牧師。ワシントン大行進では、有名な "I have a dream" の演説を行った。1964年ノーベル平和賞受賞。**segregation**「人種差別」**Augustine of Hippo**「ヒッポのアウグスティヌス（354-430）」北アフリカのヒッポ（現在のアルジェリア北東部に位置する都市アンナバ）の司教で、初期キリスト教最大の教父。**on one's behalf**「〜に代わって、〜を代表して」**universal suffrage**「普通選挙権」**sign up**「（SNSなどに）登録する」**the Eugenic Protection Law**「優生保護法」この法令のもと障害者への強制不妊手術が行われた。1996年に母体保護法に改正された。**the head of state**「（国家）元首」**a capital crime**「死刑に値する罪、死罪」

▶ Questions for Understanding

Part 1 *Look at the following statements about the passage. Write T if the statement is True, and F if it is False. Write the number of the paragraph where you find the answer in the parenthesis.*

1) ____ There are sometimes good reasons to prevent someone from voting.

( )

2) ____ In some US states a person can be old enough to get married but be too young to get divorced. ( )

3) ____ Until recently it was illegal for people from different races to get married in Japan. ( )

4) ____ The majority of countries require their citizens to follow a national religion.

( )

Part 2 *Look at the following questions about the passage. Check the best answer for each.*

1) Which word has the closest meaning to the word "obey" in Paragraph 1 (line 7)?
a. ☐ follow   b. ☐ challenge   c. ☐ defy   d. ☐ violate

2) Why was Martin Luther King Jr. arrested in 1963?
a. ☐ Because he wanted to vote in an election in Birmingham, Alabama.
b. ☐ Because he had been sent a letter from the Birmingham jail.
c. ☐ Because he was trying to end racial inequality in the United States.
d. ☐ Because he had recently changed his religion and become a Christian.

3) What proportion of women are married under the age of 18?
a. ☐ About one fifth
b. ☐ About one quarter
c. ☐ About one third
d. ☐ About half

4) Why do the majority of countries restrict the right to free speech?

    a. ☐ Because it is important to protect the leaders of a country from insult.

    b. ☐ Because it is necessary to prevent people from misusing free speech.

    c. ☐ Because it is essential for everybody to follow the official religion.

    d. ☐ Because it is vital to limit the information available to the people.

❯ Summary

② 89

Fill each space with the best word from the list below.

degrades	consequently	sterilized
available	affected	consent

The politicians that we elect make laws on our behalf. Naturally, we are all **1)** _____ by those laws, whether they are good or bad. So how can we tell a bad law from a good one? Bad laws have been used to limit the amount of information people have **2)** _____ and to limit their choice of religion. Other bad laws have been based on the incorrect ideas of eugenics and resulted in thousands of people being **3)** _____. A bad law is one which **4)** _____ our rights or our ability to ask questions about ideas or people. **5)** _____, in order to protect ourselves and our society, it is important to make sure that we only give our **6)** _____ to laws that are good.

❯ Over to You

Choose ONE of the statements below. Prepare a short response giving your opinion.

> • **Bad laws are not really a problem if people are good.**
> • **We should always be suspicious of the government.**

....

....

....

....

Compiled References by Chapter

Many references were consulted in writing this book. The following is a list of the most useful, and we direct students and teachers who are interested in learning more about the issues raised in this book to them.

Culture and Society

Chapter 1   I Can't Believe My Eyes – Finding Truth in a Virtual World

- BBC News. (2019, October 23). Alexander McCartney: 'Thousands of new victims' found in child abuse case. *BBC News*. https://www.bbc.com/news/uk-northern-ireland-50157804
- BBC News. (2019, May 23). Facebook: Another three billion fake profiles culled. *BBC News*. https://www.bbc.com/news/technology-48380504
- Buchanan, T. & Whitty, M.T. (2013). The online dating romance scam: Causes and consequences of victimhood. *Psychology, Crime & Law, 20*(3), 261-283. http://dx.doi.org/10.1080/1068316X.2013.772180
- Fletcher, E. (2019, February 12). Romance scams rank number one on total reported losses. *Federal Trade Commission*. https://www.ftc.gov/news-events/blogs/data-spotlight/2019/02/romance-scams-rank-number-one-total-reported-losses
- Normille, D. (2017, November 30). Q&A: Japanese physician snares prize for battling antivaccine campaigners. *Science*. https://www.sciencemag.org/news/2017/11/qa-japanese-physician-snares-prize-battling-antivaccine-campaigners
- Sagan, C. (1979). *Broca's Brain*. Presidio Press.
- van den Brink-Budgen, R. (2010). *Critical Thinking for Students* (4th ed.). How To Books.

Chapter 2   It's a Hikikomori World – Why Do Some People Withdraw from Society?

- Kyodo. (2019, March 29) 613,000 in Japan aged 40 to 64 are recluses, says first government survey of hikikomori. *The Japan Times*. https://www.japantimes.co.jp/news/2019/03/29/national/613000-japan-aged-40-64-recluses-says-first-government-survey-hikikomori/
- Crystal, D.S., Kakinuma, M., DeBell, M., Azuma, H. & Miyashita, T. (2008). Who helps you? Self and other sources of support among youth in Japan and the USA. *International Journal of Behavioral Development, 32*(6), 496-508.
- Hoffman, M. (2011, October 9). Nonprofits in Japan help 'shut-ins' get out into the open. *The Japan Times*. https://www.japantimes.co.jp/news/2011/10/09/national/media-national/nonprofits-in-japan-help-shut-ins-get-out-into-the-open/
- Kato, T.A., Kanba, S. & Teo, A.R. (2018). Hikikomori: Experience in Japan and international relevance. *World Psychiatry, 17*(1), 105-106.
- Kremer, W. & Hammond, C. (2013, July 5). Hikikomori: Why are so many Japanese men refusing to leave their rooms? *BBC News*. https://www.bbc.com/news/magazine-23182523
- Pozza, A., Coluccia, A., Kato, T., Gaetani, M., & Ferretti, F. (2019). The 'Hikikomori' syndrome: Worldwide prevalence and co-occurring major psychiatric disorders: a systematic review and meta-analysis protocol. *BMJOpen, 9* (9), e025213. http://dx.doi.org/10.1136/bmjopen-2018-025213
- Merriam-Webster. (n.d). *Instagram*. Merriam-Webster. https://www.merriam-webster.com/dictionary/instagram
- Yong, R. & Nomura, K. (2019). Hikikomori Is Most Associated with Interpersonal Relationships, Followed by Suicide Risks: A Secondary Analysis of a National Cross-Sectional Study. *Frontiers in Psychiatry, 10*: 247. https://www.frontiersin.org/articles/10.3389/fpsyt.2019.00247/full

Chapter 3   Not Just for Fun – The Importance of Play and Games

- Barblett, L., Knaus, M., & Barratt-Pugh, C. (2016). The pushes and pulls of pedagogy in the early years: Competing knowledges and the erosion of play-based learning. *Australasian Journal of Early Childhood, 41*(4), 36-43.
- Cohen, D. (2006). *The development of play (3rd ed.)*. New York University Press.
- Ginsberg, K.R. (2007). The importance of play in promoting healthy child development and maintaining strong parent-child bonds. *American Academy of Pediatrics, 119*(1), 182-191. https://doi.org/10.1542/peds.2006-2697

- Hunkin, E. (2014). We're offering true play-based learning: Teacher perspectives on educational dis/continuity in the early years. *Australasian Journal of Early Childhood, 39*(2), 30–35.
- Krantcents. (2010, December 27). The Importance of playing games. *Krantcents: Making Sense of Money*. https://www.krantcents.com/the-importance-of-playing-games/
- McInnes, K., Howard, J., Crowley, K., & Miles, G. (2013). The nature of adult–child interaction in the early years classroom: Implications for children's perceptions of play and subsequent learning behaviour. *European Early Childhood Education Research Journal, 21*(2), 268–282. https://doi.org/10.1080/1350293X.2013.789194
- National Literacy Trust. (2017, August 25). 10 Reasons why play is important. *National Literary Trust*. https://literacytrust.org.uk/resources/10-reasons-why-play-important/
- Robinson, L., Smith, M., Segal, J., & Shubin, J. (n.d.). The benefits of play for adults. *Help Guide: Your Trusted Guide to Mental Health & Wellness*. https://www.helpguide.org/articles/mental-health/benefits-of-play-for-adults.htm
- Singer, D., & Singer, J. L. (2005). *Imagination and play in the electronic age*. Cambridge, MA: Harvard University Press.
- Singer, D., Golinkoff, R., & Hirsh-Pasek, K. (2006). *Play equals learning: How play motivates and enhances children's cognitive and socio-emotional growth*. New York, NY: Oxford University Press.
- Tsao, L. (2002). How much do we know about the importance of play in child development? *Child Education, 78*, 230 - 233.

Chapter 4   See It While You Can – The Risks of Over-Tourism
- BBC News. (2019, October 1). Komodo: Tourists must pay $1,000 to enter 'Dragon Island.' *BBC News*. https://www.bbc.com/news/world-asia-49888876
- BBC News. (2019, October 25). Uluru climbing ban: Tourists scale sacred rock for final time. *BBC News*. https://www.bbc.com/news/world-australia-50151344
- CNT Editors. (2018, October 24). 15 Beloved places struggling with overtourism. *Conde Nast Traveler*. https://www.cntraveler.com/galleries/2015-06-19/barcelona-bhutan-places-that-limit-tourist-numbers
- Green Global Travel. (n.d.). The effects of mass tourism (How overtourism is destroying 30+ destinations). *Green Global Travel*. https://greenglobaltravel.com/effects-mass-tourism-overtourism-destroying-destinations/
- Jet, J. (2018, August 20). How is overtourism impacting travel to popular destinations? *Forbes*. https://www.forbes.com/sites/johnnyjet/2018/08/20/how-is-overtourism-impacting-travel-to-popular-destinations/#36ecb3ac35b8
- Gordon, Y. (2017, August 31). Lisbon's 'we hate tourism' tours teach visitors how to travel responsibly. *The Independent*. http://www.independent.co.uk/travel/europe/lisbon-tourists-we-hate-tourismtours-locals-responsible-travel-portugal-a7919571.html
- Paris, N. (2017, August 8). Tourists have turned Oxford into 'hell', locals claim. *The Telegraph*. http://www.telegraph.   co.uk/travel/news/oxford-tourist-hell-overcrowding-residents-locals-complain
- Seraphin, H., Sheeran, P., & Pilato, M. (2018) Over-tourism and the fall of Venice as a destination. *Journal of Destination Marketing Management, 9*, 374-376.
- Singh, T. (2018). Is over-tourism the downside of mass tourism? *Tourism Recreation Research, 43*(4), 415-416.

Chapter 5   The World's Greatest Gamers – The Rise of Esports
- Baseel, C. (2019, September 18). Japan's first dedicated esports hotel to open next spring with three full floors of gaming gear. *Japan Today*. https://japantoday.com/category/features/lifestyle/japan%E2%80%99s-first-dedicated-esports-hotel-to-open-next-spring-with-three-full-floors-of-gaming-gear
- Jacobs, H. (2015, May 12). Here's the insane training schedule of a 20-something professional gamer. *Business Insider*. https://www.businessinsider.com/pro-gamers-explain-the-insane-training-regimen-they-use-to-stay-on-top-2015-5
- Kari, T. & Karhulahti, V. (2016). Do e-athletes move? A study on training and physical exercise in

elite e-sports. *International Journal of Gaming and Computer-Mediated Simulations, 8*(4), 53-66.

· Kosik, A. H. (2018, February 12). How much do Olympic athletes train in a day? It's every bit as intense as you think", *Bustle*. https://www.bustle.com/p/how-much-do-olympic-athletes-train-in-a-day-its-every-bit-as-intense-as-you-think-7942978

· Nagesh, A. (2019, August 20). The International 2019: What does it take to become a gaming millionaire? *BBC News*. https://www.bbc.com/news/world-49206676

· Nakamura, Y., Nobuhiro, E. & Taniguchi, T. (2018, January 19). Shinzo Abe's party wants Japan ready for video games in Olympics. *Bloomberg*. https://www.bloomberg.com/news/articles/2018-01-18/shinzo-abe-s-party-wants-japan-ready-for-video-games-in-olympics

· Russ, H. (2019, February 13). Global esports revenues to top $1 billion in 2019: Report. *Reuters*. https://www.reuters.com/article/us-videogames-outlook-idUSKCN1Q11XY

· Stanton, R. (2015, May 29). The secret to esports athletes' success? Lots -- and lots -- of practice. *ESPN*. https://www.espn.com/espn/story/_/id/13053116/esports-athletes-put-hours-training-reach-pinnacle

· Tidy, J. (2019, July 28). Fortnite: UK player finishes second in e-sports World Cup", *BBC News*. https://www.bbc.com/news/technology-49141738

· Tidy, J. (2019, August 17). The Fortnite coach who helped create teenage millionaires. *BBC News*. https://www.bbc.com/news/technology-49374856

· Tidy, J. (2019, July 28). US teenager wins $3m as Fortnite world champion. *BBC News*. https://www.bbc.com/news/technology-49146644

· Wikipedia. (n.d). *Esports. Wikipedia*. https://en.wikipedia.org/wiki/Esports

· Wikipedia. (n.d). *Spacewar! Wikipedia*. https://en.wikipedia.org/wiki/Spacewar!

· Wikipedia. (n.d). *The International (Dota 2). Wikipedia*. https://en.wikipedia.org/wiki/The_International_(Dota_2)

· Wikipedia. (n.d). *Twitch.tv. Wikipedia*. https://en.wikipedia.org/wiki/Twitch.tv

Science and Technology
Chapter 6   3D-Printed Limbs and Robot Doctors – Amazing Advances in Medicine

· Arias Vázquez, P. I., et al. (2018). Prevalence and correlations between suicide attempt, depression, substance use, and functionality among patients with limb amputations. *International Journal of Rehabilitation Research, 41*(1), 52-56.

· Baraniuk, C. (2019, November 22). An AI doctor is analysing heart scans in dozens of hospitals. *New Scientist, 3258.*

· CDC. (n.d.). Facts about upper and lower limb reduction defects. *Centers for Disease Control and Prevention*. https://www.cdc.gov/ncbddd/birthdefects/ul-limbreductiondefects.html

· Crane, L. (2020, January 21). Electrified artificial skin can feel exactly where it is touched. *New Scientist*, 3266.

· Goldfarb, C. A., Shaw, N., Steffen, J. A., & Wall, L. B. (2017). The prevalence of congenital hand and upper extremity anomalies based upon the New York Congenital Malformations Registry. *Journal of Pediatric Orthopedics, 37*(2), 144-148.

· Hero Arm (n.d.). *OpenBionics*. https://openbionics.com/

· Le, J.T. et al. (2015). Pediatric limb differences and amputations. *Physical Medicine and Rehabilitation Clinics, 26*(1), 95-108.

· Le Page, M. (2019, June 26). AIs that diagnose diseases are starting to assist and replace doctors. *New Scientist, 3236.*

· Le Page, M. (2019, July 4). Five couples lined up for CRISPR babies to avoid deafness. *New Scientist, 3238.*

· Psyonic. (n.d.). *Psyonic*. http://www.psyonic.co/abilityhand

· Raichle, K. A., Hanley, M. A., Molton, I., Kadel, N. J., Campbell, K., Phelps, E., Ehde, D., Smith, D. G. (2008). Prosthesis use in persons with lower- and upper-limb amputation. *Journal of Rehabilitation Research and Development, 45*(7), 961-972.

· Roser, M., Ortiz-Ospina, E. & Ritchie, H. (2020). Life expectancy. *OurWorldInData.org*. https://ourworldindata.org/life-expectancy

· Wilson, C. (2019, September 9). An artificial leg with sensors helps people feel every step. *New*

Scientist, 3247.

- Ye, Y. (2019, May 23). Robots conduct daily health inspections of schoolchildren in China. *New Scientist, 3232.*

Chapter 7   Fake Burgers and Electric Gum – The Future of Food

- Adam, D. (2019, July 20). The super fly that could feed us, end waste and make plastic and fuel. *New Scientist, 3239.*
- BBC News. (2019, August 27). KFC to trial plant-based nuggets and wings in US. *BBC News.* https://www.bbc.com/news/business-49479220
- BBC News. (2019, June 28). New Zealand 'fake meat' pizza was not misleading, says Hell Pizza. *BBC News.* https://www.bbc.com/news/world-asia-48796006
- FAO, IFAD, UNICEF, WFP & WHO. (2019). *The State of Food Security and Nutrition in the World 2019. Safeguarding against economic slowdowns and downturns.* FAO.
- FAO. (2018). *Food loss and waste and the right to adequate food: making the connection.* FAO.
- Firth, N. (2018, May 5). The fake burger test: Could meat made of plants ever fool you? *New Scientist, 3176.*
- Matveeva, T.V. & Otten, L. (2019). Widespread occurrence of natural genetic transformation of plants by *Agrobacterium. Plant Molecular Biology, 101*(4-5), 415-437.
- Page, M. L. (2018, May 26). There's a new kind of superfood – and it's not what you think. *New Scientist, 3179.*
- Patton, L., Shanker, D. & Rockeman, O. (2019, August 2). Impossible burgers touching beef Whoppers have vegans on alert. *Bloomberg.* https://www.bloomberg.com/news/articles/2019-08-01/impossible-burgers-touching-beef-whoppers-have-vegans-on-alert
- Revell, T. (2018, October 20). Electric chewing gum zaps your tongue to create a virtual flavour hit. *New Scientist, 3200.*
- Taylor, K. (2019, September 26). McDonald's is testing a veggie burger made with Beyond Meat, but it isn't 100% vegan. *Business Insider.* https://www.businessinsider.com/mcdonalds-beyond-meat-burger-test-not-100-percent-vegan-2019-9
- Zsögön, A., Čermák, T., Naves, E. et al. (2018). De novo domestication of wild tomato using genome editing. *Nature Biotechnology, 36*, 1211-1216.

Chapter 8   The Sports Space Race – The Impact of Science in Sports

- Agrawal, A.J. (2015, December 21). 3 ways technology has changed the sports industry. *inc.* https://www.inc.com/aj-agrawal/3-ways-technology-has-changed-the-sports-industry.html
- Axisa, M. (2019, March 18). MLB is working on a system that will allow pitchers and catchers to communicate through watches. *CBS Sports.* https://www.cbssports.com/mlb/news/mlb-is-working-on-a-system-that-will-allow-pitchers-and-catchers-to-communicate-through-watches/
- Lee, D. (2015, January 13). Tennis racquet technology comes with strings attached. *BBC News.* https://www.bbc.com/news/business-30746221
- Loria, K. (2015, August 12). Science is creating super-athletes – and making sports unrecognizable to previous generations. *Business Insider.* https://www.businessinsider.com/how-science-and-technology-are-changing-sports-2015-8
- Timmer, J. (2018, November 11). How bicycles have changed in the last 25 years. *ars Technica.* https://arstechnica.com/gadgets/2018/11/25-years-of-two-wheeled-tech/
- Topend Sports. (n.d.). Sport Science Disciplines. *Topend Sports.* https://www.topendsports.com/science.htm
- Woodford, C. (2019, February 17). The Science of Sport. *Explainthatstuff.* https://www.explainthatstuff.com/science-of-sport.html

Chapter 9   Turn the Lights Out – What Is Light Pollution?

- Carter, J. (2018, October 18). China's 'Fake Moons' could make light pollution 50 times worse, warns astronomer. *Forbes.* https://www.forbes.com/sites/jamiecartereurope/2018/10/18/chinas-fake-moons-could-make-light-pollution-almost-fifty-times-worse-warns-astronomer/#2a4c54715cf2
- Drake, N. (2019, April 3). Our Nights are getting brighter, and Earth is paying the price. *National*

Geographic. https://www.nationalgeographic.com/science/2019/04/nights-are-getting-brighter-earth-paying-the-price-light-pollution-dark-skies/
- Griffiths, S. (2019, September 19). The manmade 'stars' changing the night sky. *BBC Future*. http://www.bbc.com/future/story/20190918-is-humanity-changing-the-night-sky-with-artificial-stars
- International Dark-Sky Association. (n.d.). First international dark sky place established in Japan. *International Dark-Sky Association*. https://www.darksky.org/first-international-dark-sky-place-established-in-japan/
- International Dark-Sky Association. (n.d.). Light pollution. *International Dark-Sky Association*. https://www.darksky.org/light-pollution/
- MacKenzie, D. (2015, December 26). As lights block out the night sky, help measure the damage. *New Scientist*. https://www.newscientist.com/article/dn28701-as-lights-block-out-the-night-sky-help-measure-the-damage/
- Nathanson, J.A. (2010, January 22). Light pollution. *Encyclopaedia Britannica*. https://www.britannica.com/science/light-pollution
- Snedeker, R. (2019, July 30). Nighttime riders navigate glowing bike paths in Poland, Holland. *Patheos*. https://www.patheos.com/blogs/godzooks/2019/07/glowing-bike-path-poland-holland/

Chapter 10   It's Good to be Grumpy – The Positive Consequences of Negative Feelings
- BBC News. (2009, November 5). Feeling grumpy is 'good for you.' *BBC News*. http://news.bbc.co.uk/2/hi/health/8339647.stm
- David, S. (2016, August 22). Don't worry, be gloomy: Negative feelings have benefits too. *Health*. https://www.health.com/mind-body/negativity-benefits
- Gorvett, Z. (2016, August 11). Why it pays to be grumpy and bad-tempered. *BBC Future*. http://www.bbc.com/future/story/20160809-why-it-pays-to-be-grumpy-and-bad-tempered
- Lafata, A. (2014, December 19). 7 emotions that actually have really positive effects on your life. *Elite daily*. https://www.elitedaily.com/life/negative-emotions-good-for-you/881761
- Liu, J. (2004). Concept analysis: Aggression. *Issues in Mental Health Nursing, 25*(7), 693-714. https://doi.org/10.1080/01612840490486755
- Neil, B. (2012, January 27). The grumpiest man in Britain. *Mirror*. https://www.mirror.co.uk/news/uk-news/the-grumpiest-man-in-britain-227208
- Reynolds, M. (2017, November 12). Can bad emotions be good for you: How to put your bad emotions to good use. *Psychology Today*. https://www.psychologytoday.com/intl/blog/wander-woman/201711/can-bad-emotions-be-good-you
- Shpancer, N. (2010, September 8). Emotional acceptance: Why feeling bad is good. *Psychology Today*. https://www.psychologytoday.com/us/blog/insight-therapy/201009/emotional-acceptance-why-feeling-bad-is-good

Business and Economics
Chapter 11   A Full Working Week – How Long Should We Work?
- Cohut, M. (2019, June 21). An 8-hour work week could be ideal for mental health. *Medical News Today*. https://www.medicalnewstoday.com/articles/325529.php#6
- Greene, J. (n.d.). Is 40 hours a week too much? Here's what history and science say. *Spoke*. https://www.askspoke.com/blog/hr/40-hour-work-week/
- International Labour Organization. (n.d.). International labour standards on working time. *International Labour Organization*. https://www.ilo.org/global/standards/subjects-covered-by-international-labour-standards/working-time/lang--en/index.htm
- Merle, A. (2018, June 11). This is how many hours you should really be working. *Medium*. https://medium.com/@andrewmerle/this-is-how-many-hours-you-should-really-be-working-ff1e8a6ad958
- Messenger, J. (2018). Working time and the future of work. *International Labour Organization*. https://www.ilo.org/wcmsp5/groups/public/---dgreports/---cabinet/documents/publication/wcms_649907.pdf
- Saiidi, U. (2018, June 1). Japan has some of the longest working hours in the world. It's trying to change. *CNBC*. https://www.cnbc.com/2018/06/01/japan-has-some-of-the-longest-working-

hours-in-the-world-its-trying-to-change.html
- Smith, N. (2019, November 11). Four-day work week could be just what Japan needs. *The Japan Times*. https://www.japantimes.co.jp/news/2019/11/11/business/four-day-workweek-just-japan-needs/#.XfiIF2QzaUk
- Stillman, J. (2017, August 29). This is the ideal number of hours to work a day, according to decades of science. *inc*. https://www.inc.com/jessica-stillman/this-is-the-ideal-number-of-hours-to-work-a-day-ac.html
- William, D.K. (n.d.). 10 reasons you should stop working long hours today. *Lifehack*. https://www.lifehack.org/articles/productivity/10-reasons-you-should-stop-working-long-hours-today.html

Chapter 12   Waste Not, Want Not – From Recycling to a Circular Economy
- Altria, L. (2019, July 9). The burning problem of Japan's waste disposal. *Tokyo Review*. https://www.tokyoreview.net/2019/07/burning-problem-japan-waste-recycling/
- Echeverria, C.A., Handoko, W., Pahlevani, F. & Sahajwalla, V. (2019). Cascading use of textile waste for the advancement of fibre reinforced composites for building applications. *Journal of Cleaner Production, 208*, 1524-1536.
- EPA. (n.d.). *Facts and Figures about Materials, Waste and Recycling*. United States Environmental Protection Agency. https://www.epa.gov/facts-and-figures-about-materials-waste-and-recycling/national-overview-facts-and-figures-materials
- Gürtler, C. & Stute, A. (2016, January). *CO_2 as a feedstock for polymers*. SETIS Magazine. https://setis.ec.europa.eu/publications/setis-magazine/carbon-capture-utilisation-and-storage/co2-feedstock-polymers
- Huotari, N., Tillman-Sutela, E., Moilanen, M. & Laiho, R. (2015). Recycling of ash – For the good of the environment? *Forest Ecology and Management, 348*, 226-240.
- Kalinowska-Wichrowska, K., Pawluczuk, E. & Bołtryk, M. (2020). Waste-free technology for recycling concrete rubble. *Construction and Building Materials, 234*. https://reader.elsevier.com/reader/sd/pii/S0950061819328594?token=3C05CFF8352635D327240169CB0E819B0F377CD41E6FD899B01F114856DE0AB5DAD3DB1A6EE0EDEE46AF1524E37F1DE9
- Klein, A. (2018, November 3). Your old, unwanted clothes can be turned into building materials. *New Scientist, 3203*.
- Knapp, B. & Insam, H. (2011). *Recycling of Biomass Ashes*. Springer Science & Business Media.
- Lawton, G. (2018, November 7). Finland's long, hard road to creating a circular economy. *New Scientist, 3203*.
- Le Page, M. (2020, January 10). Can we really save the planet by making food 'from air' without farms? *New Scientist, 3265*.
- WEF. (2020). *The Global Risks Report 2020*. World Economic Forum.

Chapter 13   Try This – Why Giving Things Away Can Be Good for Business
- Hardoon, A. (2014, February 13). Seven benefits of giving out free samples. *Small Business*. https://smallbusiness.co.uk/seven-benefits-of-giving-out-free-samples-2453977/
- O'Shaughnessy, E. (n.d.). 6 reasons giving away free stuff can work for your small business. *Ideas 4 smallbiz*. http://ideas4smallbiz.com/2012/04/6-reasons-giving-away-free-stuff-can-work-for-your-small-business/
- Shimp, T. A., (2007). *Advertising, promotion, and other aspects of integrated marketing communications (7th ed.)*. Thompson South-West.
- White, M.C. (2013, June 24). 5 ways companies win by giving stuff away. *Time*. http://business.time.com/2013/06/24/5-ways-companies-win-by-giving-stuff-away/

Chapter 14   Selling Sports – The Commercialization of Sports
- Austin, S. & Jacobson, L. (2019, July 11). "Does the U.S. women's soccer team bring in more revenue but get paid less than the men? *Politifact*. https://www.politifact.com/truth-o-meter/article/2019/jul/11/does-us-womens-soccer-team-bring-more-revenue-get-/
- Badenhausen, K. (2019, July 22). The world's 50 most valuable sports' teams. *Forbes*. https://www.forbes.com/sites/kurtbadenhausen/2019/07/22/the-worlds-50-most-valuable-sports-teams-

2019/#b5fc928283da

- BBC News. (2020, February 5). Cristiano Ronaldo: South Korean fans compensated after Juventus forward fails to play. *BBC News*. https://www.bbc.com/sport/football/51372201
- BBC News. (2019, July 30). Cristiano Ronaldo: Fans seek lawsuit after South Korea no-show. *BBC News*. https://www.bbc.com/news/world-asia-49168694
- BBC News. (2019, March 8). US women's national team take legal action over discrimination. *BBC News*. https://www.bbc.com/sport/football/47502225
- Egan, J. (2008). *Relationship Marketing*. Pearson.
- Handley, L. (2018, September 25). Sponsorship spending to hit $66 billion worldwide, but most firms don't know if it really works. *CNBC*. https://www.cnbc.com/2018/09/25/does-sponsorship-work-deals-value-to-reach-66-billion-in-2018.html
- Houlihan, B. & White, A. (2002). *The Politics of Sports Development: Development of Sport or Development Through Sport?* Routledge.
- Hubman, J. (2011). A Financial Analysis of Publicly Traded Professional Sports Teams. *Senior Honors Theses*. 69. https://pdfs.semanticscholar.org/54c4/4e51f356a6c60f5c8c1470fd332ba4e1e554.pdf
- McAllister, M. P. (2010). Hypercommercialism, televisuality, and the changing nature of college sports sponsorship. *American Behavioral Scientist, 53*(10), 1476-1491.
- Mouritsen, H. (2001). *Plebs and Politics in the Late Roman Republic*. Cambridge University Press.
- Schaaff, P. (2004). *Sports Inc*. Prometheus Books.
- World Atlas. (n.d). *The 10 most expensive stadiums in the world*. World Atlas. https://www.worldatlas.com/articles/the-10-most-expensive-stadiums-in-the-world.html

Chapter 15   Paying for Information – The Cost of News

- Arns, T. (2018, August 26). Japanese publisher Mainichi uses Cxense to build digital subscription business. Cxense. https://www.cxense.com/blog/japanese-publisher-mainichi-uses-cxense-build-digital-subscription-business
- Baek, H., Ahn, J., & Choi, Y. (2012). Helpfulness of online consumer reviews: Readers' objectives and review cues. *International Journal of Electronic Commerce, 17*(2), 99-126.
- Benton, A. (2018). So some people will pay for a subscription to a news site. How about two? Three? *Nieman Lab*. https://www.niemanlab.org/2018/11/so-some-people-will-pay-for-a-subscription-to-a-news-site-how-about-two-three/
- Dwivedi, Y. K., Kapoor, K. K., & Chen, H. (2015). Social media marketing and advertising. *The Marketing Review, 15*(3), 289-309.
- Else, H. (2019, February 5). Thousands of scientists run up against Elsevier's paywall. *Nature*. https://www.nature.com/articles/d41586-019-00492-4
- Farooqi, A. (2019, June 17). Next Chrome release will making bypassing paywalls easier. *Ubergizmo*.https://www.ubergizmo.com/2019/06/next-chrome-release-will-making-bypassing-paywalls-easier/
- Hendrickson, C. (2018, January 4). Paywalls & publishers part 3: Paywall models. *Marfeel*. https://www.marfeel.com/blog/paywalls-publishers-part-3-an-analysis-of-paywall-models/
- Horn, L. (2002). Making trade shows pay off. *Journal of Promotion Management, 8*(1), 127-136.
- Lever, R. (2018, February 26). Free news gets scarcer as paywalls tighten. *Japan Today*. https://japantoday.com/category/business/free-news-gets-scarcer-as-paywalls-tighten
- Mitchell, D. & Coles, C. (2004). Business model innovation breakthrough moves. *Journal of Business Strategy, 25*(1), 16-26.
- Sawa, Y. (2018). Digital news report. *Reuters*. http://www.digitalnewsreport.org/survey/2018/japan-2018/
- Senz, K. (2019, August 1). Why paywalls aren't always the answer for newspapers. *Forbes*. https://www.forbes.com/sites/hbsworkingknowledge/2019/08/01/why-paywalls-arent-always-the-answer-for-newspapers/#2abd94dc429f

Politics and International Relations
Chapter 16   Your Phone Is a Soldier – What Does Cyberwar Mean?
- Alperovitch, D. (2011). *Revealed: Operation Shady RAT*. MacAfee Inc.

- Anderson, N. (2012, June 1). Confirmed: US and Israel created Stuxnet, lost control of it. *Ars Technica*. https://arstechnica.com/tech-policy/2012/06/confirmed-us-israel-created-stuxnet-lost-control-of-it/
- Ball, J. (2019, February 23). Russia's plan to unplug from the internet shows cyberwar is escalating. *New Scientist, 3218.*
- Bumgarner, J. (2010). Computers as Weapons of War. *IO Journal, 2*(2), 4-8.
- Chin, W. (2019). Technology, war and the state: past, present and future. *International Affairs, 95*(4), 765-783.
- German, T. (2019). Re-visioning war and the state in the twenty-first century. *International Affairs, 95*(4), 759-763.
- Gibbs, S. (2017, December 15). Triton: hackers take out safety systems in 'watershed' attack on energy plant. *The Guardian*. https://www.theguardian.com/technology/2017/dec/15/triton-hackers-malware-attack-safety-systems-energy-plant
- Greenberg, A. (2019, June 14). The highly dangerous 'Triton' hackers have probed the US grid. *Wired*. https://www.wired.com/story/triton-hackers-scan-us-power-grid/
- Greenberg, A. (2017, June 20). How an entire nation became Russia's test lab for cyberwar. *Wired*. https://www.wired.com/story/russian-hackers-attack-ukraine/
- Halpern, M. (2015, April 22). Iran flexes its power by transporting Turkey to the Stone Age. *Observer*. https://observer.com/2015/04/iran-flexes-its-power-by-transporting-turkey-to-the-stone-ages/
- Hambling, D. (2017, August 17). Ships fooled in GPS spoofing attack suggest Russian cyberweapon. *New Scientist, 3139.*
- Hern, A. (2018, January 28). Fitness tracking app Strava gives away location of secret US army bases. *The Guardian*. https://www.theguardian.com/world/2018/jan/28/fitness-tracking-app-gives-away-location-of-secret-us-army-bases
- Machkovech, S. (2015, April 10). Hacked French network exposed its own passwords during TV interview. *Ars Technica*. https://arstechnica.com/information-technology/2015/04/hacked-french-network-exposed-its-own-passwords-during-tv-interview/
- Select Committee on Intelligence. (2017). *Russian Interference in the 2016 U.S. Elections*. Select Committee on Intelligence. US Government Publishing Office.
- von Clausewitz, C. (2008). *On War*. Oxford University Press.
- Wikipedia. (n.d.). *Cyberwarfare. Wikipedia*. https://en.wikipedia.org/wiki/Cyberwarfare

Chapter 17   The Perils of Perception – Why We Need to Know More About Everything
- Aron, J. (2019, September 4). The world is getting better, so why are we convinced otherwise? *New Scientist, 3246.*
- BBC News. (2014, December 4). Russia: 'Good news day' decimates website's readership. *BBC News*. https://www.bbc.com/news/blogs-news-from-elsewhere-30318261
- Davies, N. (2008). *Flat Earth News*. Vintage Books.
- Duffy, B. (2018). *The Perils of Perception*. Atlantic Books.
- Hooton, C. (2014, December 5). Website reports only good news for a day, loses two thirds of its readers. *The Independent*. https://www.independent.co.uk/news/world/europe/website-reports-only-good-news-for-a-day-loses-two-thirds-of-its-readers-9905916.html
- Kahan, D.M. (2010). Fixing the communications failure. *Nature, 463*, 296-297.
- McHugh, D. (2020, January 6). Global air crash deaths fall by more than half in 2019. *Manufacturing.net*. https://www.manufacturing.net/aerospace/news/21108682/global-air-crash-deaths-fall-by-more-than-half-in-2019
- Westmorland, D. & McCormick, C. (2020, January 8). Embracing flat Earth science denialism can help us overcome it. *New Scientist, 3264.*

Chapter 18   It's a Man's World – The Cost of Ignoring Women's Needs
- BBC News. (2020, April 29). PPE 'designed for women' needed on frontline. *BBC News*. https://www.bbc.com/news/health-52454741
- BBC News. (2019, August 7). Zuleika Hassan: Kenyan MP with baby ordered to leave parliament. *BBC News*. https://www.bbc.com/news/world-africa-49266396

- Bratberg, E., Dahl, S., & Risa, A.E. (2002). 'The double burden': Do combinations of career and family obligations increase sickness absence among women? *European Sociological Review, 18*(2), 233-249.
- Crane, L. (2019, March 30). NASA cancels first all-women spacewalk due to spacesuit size issue. *New Scientist, 3223*.
- Criado-Perez, C. (2019, February 23). The deadly truth about a world built for men – from stab vests to car crashes. *The Guardian*. https://www.theguardian.com/lifeandstyle/2019/feb/23/truth-world-built-for-men-car-crashes
- Geiger, D. & Antonacopoulou, E. (2009). Narratives and organizational dynamics: Exploring blind spots and organizational inertia. *The Journal of Applied Behavioral Science, 45*(3), 411-436.
- Gordon, R.A., Kaestner, R., & Korenman, S. (2008). Child care and work absences: Trade-offs by type of care. *Journal of Marriage and Family, 70*(1), 239-254.
- Lockard, C. (2014). *Societies, Networks, and Transitions: A Global History*, Cengage Learning.
- Nature Index. Lost in Japan, a generation of brilliant women. *Nature Index*. https://www.natureindex.com/news-blog/lost-in-japan-a-generation-of-brilliant-women
- Nguyen, H.L., Saczynski, J.S., Gore, J.M., & Goldberg, R.J. (2010). Age and sex differences in duration of prehospital delay in patients with acute myocardial infarction: a systematic review. *Circulation. Cardiovascular Quality and Outcomes, 3*(1), 82-92.
- Park, L.E., Young, A.F., & Eastwick, P.W. (2015). (Psychological) distance makes the heart grow fonder: Effects of psychological distance and relative intelligence on men's attraction to women. *Personality and Social Psychology Bulletin, 41*(11), 1459-1473.
- The World Bank. (n.d.). Proportion of seats held by women in national parliaments. The World Bank. https://data.worldbank.org/indicator/sg.gen.parl.zs
- Office for Gender Equality. (n.d.). The first 19 female students at Todai. University of Tokyo. https://www.u-tokyo.ac.jp/kyodo-sankaku/en/activities/model-program/library/UTW_History/Page03.html
- Workman, L. & Reader, W. (2014). *Evolutionary Psychology*. Cambridge University Press.
- World Economic Forum. (2018). *The Global Gender Gap Report 2018*. World Economic Forum.

Chapter 19 Changing Perceptions – Can a Country Change the Way It's Viewed?

- Chemonics. (2015, October 13). Changing perceptions: Boosting Jordan's international appeal. *Chemonics*. https://www.chemonics.com/impact-story/changing-perceptions-boosting-jordans-international-appeal/
- Dinnie, K. (2004). Place branding: Overview of an emerging literature. *Place Branding, 1*, 106-110. https://doi.org/10.1057/palgrave.pb.5990010
- Fabiano, G. (2016, February 2). Redefining places: How branding cities and countries can change perceptions. *Blueprint: CBRE*. https://blueprint.cbre.com/redefining-places-how-branding-cities-and-countries-can-change-perceptions/
- Gilmore, F. (2002). A country — can it be repositioned? Spain — the success story of country branding. *Journal of Brand Management, 9*, 281-293. https://doi.org/10.1057/palgrave.bm.2540078
- Gudjonsson, H. (2005). Nation branding. *Place Branding and Public Diplomacy, 1*(3), 283-298.
- Iida, T. (2018). Media coverage and the association between Japanese perceptions of South Korea and North Korea. *Japanese Political Science Review, 4*, 1.25. doi: 10.15544/2018005
- Jansen, S.C. (2008). Designer nations: Neo-liberal nation branding - Brand Estonia. *Social Identities, 14*(1), 121-142.
- Olins, W. (2002). Branding the nation - The historical context. *Journal of Brand Management, 9*(4-5), 241-248.
- van Ham, P. (2001). The rise of the Brand State. *Foreign Affairs, 80*(5), 2-6.
- van Ham, P. (2008). Place branding: The state of the art. *The Annals of the American Academy of Political and Social Science, 616*(1), 126-149.

Chapter 20 It's the Law – Identifying Good and Bad Laws

- Committee to Protect Journalists. (2015). Repressive nations threaten jail terms, restrict Internet

to silence press. *Committee to Protect Journalists*. https://cpj.org/2015/04/10-most-censored-countries.php
- Freedom House. (2019). *Freedom in the World 2019*. Freedom House.
- Hurst, D. (2019, March 18). Victims of forced sterilisation in Japan to receive compensation and apology. *The Guardian*. https://www.theguardian.com/world/2019/mar/18/victims-of-forced-sterilisation-in-japan-to-receive-compensation-and-apology
- Oppenheimer, D.B. (1993). Martin Luther King, Walker v. City of Birmingham, and the Letter from Birmingham Jail. *U.C. Davis Law Review, 26*(4), 791-833.
- Phelan, J. (2014, March 12). This is how these 12 countries will punish you for insulting their heads of state. *Public Radio International*. https://www.pri.org/stories/2014-03-12/how-these-12-countries-will-punish-you-insulting-their-heads-state
- Robertson, J. (2002). Blood talks: Eugenic modernity and the creation of new Japanese. *History and Anthropology, 13*(3), 191-216.
- Pew Research Center, (2016). *Trends in Global Restrictions on Religion*. Pew Research Center.
- Unchained At Last. (n.d.). Child marriage – Shocking statistics. *Unchained At Last*. https://www.unchainedatlast.org/child-marriage-shocking-statistics/
- United Nations. (1948). *Universal Declaration of Human Rights*, United Nations.
- United Nations Children's Fund. (2018). *Child Marriage: Latest trends and future prospects*. UNICEF.
- Wikipedia. (n.d.). Women's Suffrage. *Wikipedia*. https://en.wikipedia.org/wiki/Women%27s_suffrage
- Wikipedia. (n.d.). Anti-miscegenation laws in the United States. *Wikipedia*. https://en.wikipedia.org/wiki/Anti-miscegenation_laws_in_the_United_States

TEXT PRODUCTION STAFF

edited by	編集
Minako Hagiwara	萩原 美奈子

cover design by	表紙デザイン
Nobuyoshi Fujino	藤野 伸芳

CD PRODUCTION STAFF

narrated by	吹き込み者
Howard Colefield　(AmE)	ハワード・コルフィールド（アメリカ英語）
Karen Haedrich　(AmE)	カレン・ヘドリック（アメリカ英語）

Grand Tour – Seeing the World
新たな時代への扉

2021年1月20日　初版発行
2022年3月10日　第3刷発行

著　　者　Anthony Sellick
　　　　　James Bury
　　　　　堀内 香織

発 行 者　佐野 英一郎

発 行 所　株式会社 成 美 堂
　　　　　〒101-0052　東京都千代田区神田小川町3-22
　　　　　TEL 03-3291-2261　FAX 03-3293-5490
　　　　　https://www.seibido.co.jp

印 刷・製 本　萩原印刷株式会社

ISBN 978-4-7919-7234-0　　　　　　　　　　Printed in Japan